2014 CUMULATIVE SUPPLEMENT TO

Arrest, Search, and Investigation in North Carolina

Fourth Edition

Robert L. Farb

The School of Government at the University of North Carolina at Chapel Hill works to improve the lives of North Carolinians by engaging in practical scholarship that helps public officials and citizens understand and improve state and local government. Established in 1931 as the Institute of Government, the School provides educational, advisory, and research services for state and local governments. The School of Government is also home to a nationally ranked graduate program in public administration and specialized centers focused on information technology and environmental finance.

As the largest university-based local government training, advisory, and research organization in the United States, the School of Government offers up to 200 courses, webinars, and specialized conferences for more than 12,000 public officials each year. In addition, faculty members annually publish approximately 50 books, manuals, reports, articles, bulletins, and other print and online content related to state and local government. Each day that the General Assembly is in session, the School produces the *Daily Bulletin Online*, which reports on the day's activities for members of the legislature and others who need to follow the course of legislation.

The Master of Public Administration Program is offered in two formats. The full-time, two-year residential program serves up to 60 students annually. In 2013 the School launched MPA@UNC, an online format designed for working professionals and others seeking flexibility while advancing their careers in public service. The School's MPA program consistently ranks among the best public administration graduate programs in the country, particularly in city management. With courses ranging from public policy analysis to ethics and management, the program educates leaders for local, state, and federal governments and nonprofit organizations.

Operating support for the School of Government's programs and activities comes from many sources, including state appropriations, local government membership dues, private contributions, publication sales, course fees, and service contracts. Visit www.sog.unc.edu or call 919.966.5381 for more information on the School's courses, publications, programs, and services.

Michael R. Smith, DEAN
Thomas H. Thornburg, SENIOR ASSOCIATE DEAN
Frayda S. Bluestein, ASSOCIATE DEAN FOR FACULTY DEVELOPMENT
L. Ellen Bradley, ASSOCIATE DEAN FOR PROGRAMS AND MARKETING
Todd A. Nicolet, ASSOCIATE DEAN FOR OPERATIONS
Bradley G. Volk, ASSOCIATE DEAN FOR ADMINISTRATION

FACULTY

Whitney Afonso
Trey Allen
Gregory S. Allison
David N. Ammons
Ann M. Anderson
Maureen Berner
Mark F. Botts
Michael Crowell
Leisha DeHart-Davis
Shea Riggsbee Denning
Sara DePasquale
James C. Drennan
Richard D. Ducker
Joseph S. Ferrell
Alyson A. Grine
Norma Houston
Cheryl Daniels Howell
Jeffrey A. Hughes
Willow S. Jacobson
Robert P. Joyce
Diane M. Juffras
Dona G. Lewandowski
Adam Lovelady

James M. Markham
Christopher B. McLaughlin
Kara A. Millonzi
Jill D. Moore
Jonathan Q. Morgan
Ricardo S. Morse
C. Tyler Mulligan
Kimberly L. Nelson
David W. Owens
LaToya B. Powell
William C. Rivenbark
Dale J. Roenigk
John Rubin
Jessica Smith
Meredith Smith
Carl W. Stenberg III
John B. Stephens
Charles Szypszak
Shannon H. Tufts
Vaughn Mamlin Upshaw
Aimee N. Wall
Jeffrey B. Welty
Richard B. Whisnant

© 2014
School of Government
The University of North Carolina at Chapel Hill
First edition 1986. Fourth edition 2011.

Printed in the United States of America

18 17 16 15 14   1 2 3 4 5

ISBN 978-1-56011-765-0

♾ This publication is printed on permanent, acid-free paper in compliance with the North Carolina General Statutes.

♲ Printed on recycled paper

Contents

Chapter 3

Law of Search and Seizure

Chapter 6

Rules of Evidence in Criminal Cases

Preface

This cumulative supplement adds new or revised information and makes other changes to the 2013 supplement to the fourth edition of *Arrest, Search, and Investigation in North Carolina* (UNC School of Government, 2011). The page number references refer to the corresponding page numbers in the fourth edition. This cumulative supplement is current with statutory law and case law through June 2014, and it replaces the 2013 supplement.

I thank School of Government faculty member Jeff Welty for his review of the text and helpful comments, as well as for his written publications that assisted in preparing the supplement. I thank School of Government faculty member Jessica Smith for the case summaries included in this supplement, which are substantially similar to those set out in her *Criminal Case Compendium*, which is available at www.sog.unc.edu/casecompendium. I thank the people in the School of Government Publications Division who contributed to the supplement's production.

I welcome comments about this supplement's scope, organization, or content. Comments may be sent to me at farb@sog.unc.edu.

Robert L. Farb
Chapel Hill
August 2014

Chapter 1

An Introduction to Constitutional Law and North Carolina Criminal Law and Procedure

There are no updates to this chapter.

Chapter 2

Law of Arrest and Investigative Stops

Chapter 2

Law of Arrest and Investigative Stops

Jurisdiction (page 14)
Limits on Law Enforcement Officers' Jurisdiction (page 14)
Territorial Jurisdiction (page 14)
Private nonprofit college campus police officers (page 16)
Footnote 31 (page 16)

In *State v. Yencer*,[1] the North Carolina Supreme Court reversed the ruling of the North Carolina Court of Appeals, summarized in the book's footnote, and ruled that campus police laws, as applied to the defendant, who was arrested by a Davidson College campus police officer for impaired driving, did not violate the First Amendment's Establishment Clause. The court noted that since its ruling in *State v. Pendleton*, 339 N.C. 379 (1994), discussed in this footnote, campus police agencies were now governed under different statutes, Chapter 74G of the North Carolina General Statutes (hereinafter G.S.), which have a secular legislative purpose. See the court's opinion for its extensive analysis of the First Amendment issues, including the status of Davidson College and Chapter 74G's provisions.

Special Jurisdictional Issues (page 19)
Immigration enforcement by North Carolina law enforcement officers (page 19)

Although North Carolina has not enacted laws similar to Arizona's, the United States Supreme Court's ruling in *Arizona v. United States*, 132 S. Ct. 2492 (2012), is of general interest. Four provisions of the Arizona law were at issue. One section made failure to comply with federal alien registration requirements a state misdemeanor. A second section made it a misdemeanor for an unauthorized alien to seek or engage in work in Arizona. A third section authorized officers to arrest without a warrant a person "the officer has probable cause to believe . . . has committed any public offense that makes the person removable from the United States."[2] A fourth section provided that officers who conduct a stop, detention, or arrest must in some circumstances make efforts to verify the person's immigration status with the federal government. The Court ruled that the first three provisions were preempted by federal law but that it was improper to enjoin the fourth provision "before the state courts had an opportunity to construe it and without some showing that enforcement of the provision in fact conflicts with federal immigration law and its objectives."[3]

---

1. 365 N.C. 292 (2011).
2. *Quoting* ARIZ. REV. STAT. ANN. § 13-3883(A)(5).
3. Arizona v. United States, 132 S. Ct. at 2510.

Footnote 66 (page 20)

If an officer is not designated under federal law to perform the functions as an immigration officer, then the officer does not have the authority to detain or arrest a person subject to a civil immigration warrant absent Immigration and Customs Enforcement's express authorization or direction. Santos v. Frederick Cnty. Bd. of Comm'rs, 725 F.3d 451 (4th Cir. 2013).

Areas controlled by the federal government (page 20)

Footnote 70 (page 20)

The North Carolina Court of Appeals in *State v. Kostick*[4] ruled that a State Highway Patrol officer had jurisdiction to arrest the defendant, a non-Indian, for a DWI (driving while impaired) committed on the Cherokee reservation and that the State had the authority to try the defendant in North Carolina state courts. The court noted that pursuant to the Tribal Code of the Eastern Band of the Cherokee Indians and mutual compact agreements between the tribe and other law enforcement agencies, the North Carolina Highway Patrol has authority to patrol and enforce the motor vehicle laws of North Carolina within the Qualla boundary of the tribe, including the authority to arrest non-Indians who commit criminal offenses on the Cherokee reservation. Thus, the court concluded that North Carolina state courts have jurisdiction over the criminal offense of driving while impaired committed by a non-Indian, even when the offense and subsequent arrest occur within the Qualla boundary of the Cherokee reservation.

Legal Standards (page 25)

Introduction (page 25)

Footnote 99 (page 25)

An additional case for this footnote: State v. Atwater, ___ N.C. App. ___, 723 S.E.2d 582 (2012) (unpublished) (because the defendant did not stop his vehicle when an officer activated his blue lights, the defendant's misconduct thereafter was properly considered in determining whether reasonable suspicion supported an investigative stop, which did not occur under *Hodari D.* until the defendant finally stopped his vehicle).

Officer's Objectively Reasonable Mistake of Fact or Law in Determining Reasonable Suspicion or Probable Cause (new section to be inserted after "Objective Standard" on page 26)

Almost all courts, including the United States Supreme Court and North Carolina appellate courts, recognize that an officer's objectively reasonable mistake of fact when deciding to make an investigative stop or an arrest may still allow a court to determine that the investigative stop or arrest was reasonable under the Fourth Amendment. Examples include an officer's objectively reasonable mistake of fact about a vehicle driver's identity[5] or the identity of a person to be arrested.[6] Courts, however, are split on whether an officer's objectively reasonable mistake of law in making an investigative stop or arrest is reasonable under the Fourth Amendment. The North Carolina Supreme Court recently dealt with this issue in *State v. Heien*,[7] when the court ruled that there was reasonable suspicion for an investigative stop of a vehicle. An officer stopped a vehicle based on a non-functioning brake light. The evidence indicated that although the left brake light was operating, the right light was not. Interpreting various statutes, the North Carolina Court of Appeals ruled that a vehicle is not required to have more than one operating brake light. It concluded that because the law had not been violated, the stop was unreasonable under the Fourth Amendment. Before the North Carolina Supreme Court, the State did not appeal the court of appeals' interpretation of statutory law. Instead, the State

---

4. ___ N.C. App. ___, 755 S.E.2d 411 (2014).

5. State v. Williams, 209 N.C. App. 255 (2011). *See generally* Illinois v. Rodriguez, 497 U.S. 177 (1990); Brinegar v. United States, 338 U.S. 160 (1949).

6. Hill v. California, 401 U.S. 797 (1971). *See also* State v. Lynch, 94 N.C. App. 330 (1989).

7. 366 N.C. 271 (2012), *cert. granted*, 134 S. Ct. 1872 (2014). See also *State v. Coleman*, ___ N.C. App. ___, 743 S.E.2d 62 (2013), a post-*Heien* case ruling that an officer's mistaken belief that an anonymous tip provided reasonable suspicion to make an investigative stop for a traffic violation was not objectively reasonable.

appealed only the court's determination that the stop was unreasonable. Thus, the issue before the court was whether an officer's mistake of law may nonetheless establish reasonable suspicion to conduct a routine traffic stop. On this issue the court ruled that an officer's objectively reasonable but mistaken belief that a traffic violation has occurred can provide reasonable suspicion for a stop. Applying this standard to the facts in this case, the court found that the officer's mistake was objectively reasonable and that the stop did not violate the Fourth Amendment.

The reader should be aware that the United States Supreme Court granted the defendant's petition for certiorari to review the *Heien* ruling.[8] The Court will likely issue its ruling between late 2014 and June 2015.

The Authority to Make an Investigative Stop: Reasonable Suspicion (page 27)

> **Footnote 115** (pages 27–28)

The publication by Jeffrey B. Welty that is cited in footnote 115 was revised in May 2014 and is available at http://nccriminallaw.sog.unc.edu/wp-content/uploads/2014/05/2014-05-Traffic-Stops.pdf.

Determination of Reasonable Suspicion (page 28)

In *Navarette v. California*,[9] the United States Supreme Court, in what it termed a "close case," ruled that an officer had reasonable suspicion to make a vehicle stop based on a 911 call.[10] After a 911 caller reported that a truck had run her off the road, a police officer located the truck the caller identified and executed a traffic stop. As officers approached the truck, they smelled marijuana. A search of the truck bed revealed 30 pounds of marijuana. The defendants moved to suppress the evidence, arguing that the traffic stop violated the Fourth Amendment because the officer lacked reasonable suspicion of criminal activity. Assuming based on the court record that the 911 call was anonymous, the Court found that it bore adequate indicia of reliability, so the officer could credit the caller's account that the truck ran her off the road. The Court explained: "By reporting that she had been run off the road by a specific vehicle—a silver Ford F-150 pickup, license plate 8D94925—the caller necessarily claimed eyewitness knowledge of the alleged dangerous driving. That basis of knowledge lends significant support to the tip's reliability."[11] The Court noted that in this respect, the case contrasted with *Florida v. J.L.*,[12] where the tip did not provide a basis to conclude that the tipster had actually seen the gun reportedly possessed by the defendant. It continued: "A driver's claim that another vehicle ran her off the road, however, necessarily implies that the informant knows the other car was driven dangerously."[13] The Court noted evidence suggesting that the caller reported the incident soon after it occurred and stated, "That sort of contemporaneous report has long been treated as especially reliable."[14] Again contrasting the case with *J.L.*, the Court noted that in *J.L.* there was no indication that the tip was contemporaneous with the observation of criminal activity or made under the stress of excitement caused by a startling event. The Court determined that another indicator of veracity is the caller's use of the 911 system, which allows calls to be recorded and law enforcement to verify information about the caller. Thus, "a reasonable officer could conclude that a false tipster would think twice before using such a system . . . [and a] caller's use of the 911 system is therefore one of the relevant circumstances that, taken together, justified the officer's reliance on the information reported in the 911 call."[15] But the Court cautioned, "None of this is to suggest that tips in 911 calls are *per se* reliable."[16]

---

8. 134 S. Ct. 1872 (2014).

9. 134 S. Ct. 1683, 1689–92 (2014).

10. The Court's ruling raises questions about the continuing validity of the North Carolina cases that previously had found insufficient evidence based on an anonymous 911 caller. These cases include *State v. Blankenship*, ___ N.C. App. ___, 748 S.E.2d 616 (2013), and *State v. Peele*, 196 N.C. App. 668 (2009).

11. *Navarette*, 134 S. Ct. at 1689 (citations omitted).

12. 529 U.S. 266 (2000).

13. 134 S. Ct. at 1689.

14. *Id.*

15. *Id.* at 1690.

16. *Id.*

The Court noted that a reliable tip will justify an investigative stop only if it creates reasonable suspicion of criminal activity. It then determined that the caller's report of being run off the roadway created reasonable suspicion of an ongoing crime such as impaired driving. It stated:

> The 911 caller . . . reported more than a minor traffic infraction and more than a conclusory allegation of drunk or reckless driving. Instead, she alleged a specific and dangerous result of the driver's conduct: running another car off the highway. That conduct bears too great a resemblance to paradigmatic manifestations of drunk driving to be dismissed as an isolated example of recklessness. Running another vehicle off the road suggests lane-positioning problems, decreased vigilance, impaired judgment, or some combination of those recognized drunk driving cues. . . . And the experience of many officers suggests that a driver who almost strikes a vehicle or another object—the exact scenario that ordinarily causes "running [another vehicle] off the roadway"—is likely intoxicated. . . . As a result, we cannot say that the officer acted unreasonably under these circumstances in stopping a driver whose alleged conduct was a significant indicator of drunk driving.[17]

Special Aspects of Stopping Authority (page 43)

Investigative Stop Based on Reasonable Suspicion (page 43)

Length of Time Allowed for an Investigative Stop (page 43)

Officer's interaction with suspect after investigative stop is completed (page 44)

In *State v. Heien*,[18] the North Carolina Supreme Court affirmed a ruling of the North Carolina Court of Appeals that a valid traffic stop was not unduly prolonged and that, as a result, the defendant gave valid consent to search his vehicle after his driver's license had been returned to him. The defendant was aware that the purpose of the investigative stop had concluded, and thus further conversation between the officer and him was consensual.

Stop without Reasonable Suspicion (page 47)

Stop of Vehicle under Community Caretaking Doctrine (new section after "Public Emergencies" on page 48)

The North Carolina Court of Appeals in *State v. Smathers*[19] upheld an officer's stop of a vehicle without probable cause or reasonable suspicion under the community caretaking doctrine, which had been recognized in a different context (a search of a trunk) by the United States Supreme Court in *Cady v. Dombrowski*,[20] discussed in the book on pages 232 and 351. The officer in *Smathers* saw the defendant driving her vehicle and striking a large animal that had run onto the road, causing the vehicle to bounce and produce sparks as it scraped the road. The officer pulled behind her and activated his blue lights to stop her vehicle to ensure that she and the vehicle were okay. As it turned out, she was impaired and was later arrested for DWI. The court set forth the State's burden to satisfy the community caretaking doctrine: (1) a search or seizure under the Fourth Amendment occurred;[21] (2) an objectively reasonable basis (that is, an officer's subjective intent is not relevant) supports the community caretaking function; and (3) the public need or interest to make the stop outweighs the intrusion on a person's privacy. Included among the relevant factors in balancing the public need or interest with a person's privacy are (1) the degree of the public interest and the exigency of the situation; (2) the circumstances surrounding the seizure, including time, location, and the degree of overt authority and force displayed by an officer; and (3) the availability, feasibility, and effectiveness of alternatives to the type of intrusion actually accomplished.

---

17. *Id.* at 1691 (citations omitted).

18. ___ N.C. ___, 749 S.E.2d 278, *aff'g per curiam* ___ N.C. App. ___, 741 S.E.2d 1 (2013). Although this case is currently pending before the United States Supreme Court, with its ruling expected between late 2014 and June 2015, the case involves a different issue (reasonable mistake of law when making an investigative stop) than the ruling discussed in the text.

19. ___ N.C. App. ___, 753 S.E.2d 380 (2014).

20. 413 U.S. 433 (1973).

21. Of course, if neither a search nor seizure occurred, there is no Fourth Amendment issue to resolve.

Motor Vehicle Checkpoints, Including Driver's License and DWI Checkpoints (page 48)

In *State v. White*,[22] officers of a local law enforcement agency conducted a driver's license checkpoint, but their agency did not have a written checkpoint policy as required by G.S. 20-16.3A(a)(2a).[23] The court ruled that this statutory violation was substantial and required the suppression of evidence obtained at the checkpoint.[24]

The Arrest Procedure (page 62)

Entering Premises to Arrest (page 66)

Exigent Circumstances That Justify Entering Premises (page 69)

> ***Footnote 375*** (page 70)

The United States Supreme Court made clear in *Stanton v. Sims*[25] that "despite our emphasis in *Welsh* on the fact that the crime at issue was minor—indeed, a mere nonjailable civil offense—nothing in the opinion establishes that the seriousness of the crime is equally important *in cases of hot pursuit.*"

Completion of Custody of the Arrestee (page 74)

Detention of Defendant Arrested for Violation of Order Limiting Freedom of Movement Involving Terrorist Attack or Isolation Order for Health Reasons (new section to be inserted on page 74 after "Securing the Arrestee and Dealing with Companions of the Arrestee")

Law enforcement officers are authorized to detain a person arrested for violating an order limiting freedom of movement or access in an area designated by the state health director or local health director when the order involves a terrorist attack using nuclear, biological, or chemical agents or when confining a person for health reasons pursuant to an isolation order or quarantine. The person may be detained in the area until the initial appearance before a magistrate.[26]

Care of Minor Children Present When Adult Supervising Them Is Arrested (new section following the section immediately above)

When a law enforcement officer arrests an adult who is supervising minor children present at the time of the arrest, the minor children must be placed with a responsible adult approved by a parent or guardian of the children. If it is not possible to place the minor children in that manner within a reasonable time, the officer must contact the county department of social services.[27]

---

22. ___ N.C. App. ___, 753 S.E.2d 698 (2014).

23. A law enforcement agency may operate a checkpoint under another agency's policy, but the policy must be stated in writing. The officers in this case were not operating under another agency's policy.

24. The court rejected the State's argument that the suppression of evidence was not permitted because Chapter 20 of the General Statutes does not contain express statutory language requiring suppression of evidence for a statutory violation. The court noted that G.S. 20-16.3A(d) specifically bars the suppression of evidence for a violation of subsection (d) (placement of checkpoints), but there is no suppression prohibition for a violation of subdivision (a)(2a), which requires a written checkpoint policy. The court reasoned that these differences reflect a legislative intent to authorize suppression for a violation of subdivision (a)(2a). In any event, the court noted other cases (see below) that upheld suppression of evidence for a Chapter 20 violation despite the lack of express authorization for a court to suppress evidence. *See* State v. Buckheit, ___ N.C. App. ___, 735 S.E.2d 345 (2012) (suppressing evidence for violation of G.S. 20-16.2(a)); State v. Hatley, 190 N.C. App. 639 (2008) (similar ruling).

25. 134 S. Ct. 3, 6 (2013) (emphasis in original).

26. G.S. 15A-401(b)(4). *See also* G.S. 130A-145, -475. For pretrial release provisions concerning these matters, see G.S. 15A-534.5.

27. G.S. 15A-401(g).

Informing a Foreign National of the Right to Have Consular Official Notified (page 75)

Footnote 398 (page 75)

The United States Department of State has published a new edition (4th ed., 2014) of the manual cited in the footnote, CONSULAR NOTIFICATION AND ACCESS. It is available at www.travel.state.gov/content/travel/english/consular notification.html.

Taking DNA Samples for Certain Offenses (page 78)

The United States Supreme Court in *Maryland v. King*[28] ruled that when officers arrest a defendant based on probable cause for a "serious offense," taking and analyzing a cheek swab of the arrestee's DNA is, like fingerprinting and photographing, a legitimate police booking procedure that is reasonable under the Fourth Amendment. The Court did not define "serious offense."[29] For analysis of this case, see the blog post by School of Government faculty member Jeffrey B. Welty cited in the accompanying footnote.[30]

---

28. 133 S. Ct. 1958 (2013).

29. United States Supreme Court cases that have used the term "serious offense" in constitutionally based rulings include those that have ruled that a defendant has a Sixth Amendment right to a jury trial for a "serious offense," defined as an offense punishable by more than six months' imprisonment. Lewis v. United States, 518 U.S. 322 (1996); Blanton v. City of N. Las Vegas, 489 U.S. 538 (1989); Codispoti v. Pennsylvania, 418 U.S. 506 (1974). The Court's opinion in *Maryland v. King* did not cite these cases, so it remains uncertain what the Court meant by the term.

30. Jeff Welty, *Supreme Court Upholds Taking DNA Upon Arrest*, N.C. CRIM. L., UNC SCH. OF GOV'T BLOG (June 4, 2013), http://nccriminallaw.sog.unc.edu/?p=4294.

Chapter 2 Appendix: Case Summaries

Chapter 2 Appendix: Case Summaries

Arrests, Investigative Stops, and Related Issues (page 89)

The Authority to Make an Investigative Stop: Reasonable Suspicion (page 90)
Determination of Reasonable Suspicion (page 90)
Generally (page 90)
UNITED STATES SUPREME COURT (page 90)

Navarette v. California, 134 S. Ct. 1683, 1689, 1690, 1691 (2014). The Court, in what it termed a "close case," ruled that an officer had reasonable suspicion to make a vehicle stop based on a 911 call. After a 911 caller reported that a truck had run her off the road, a police officer located the truck the caller identified and executed a traffic stop. As officers approached the truck, they smelled marijuana. A search of the truck bed revealed 30 pounds of marijuana. The defendants moved to suppress the evidence, arguing that the traffic stop violated the Fourth Amendment because the officer lacked reasonable suspicion of criminal activity. Assuming based on the court record that the 911 call was anonymous, the Court found that it bore adequate indicia of reliability, so the officer could credit the caller's account that the truck ran her off the road. The Court explained: "By reporting that she had been run off the road by a specific vehicle—a silver Ford F-150 pickup, license plate 8D94925—the caller necessarily claimed eyewitness knowledge of the alleged dangerous driving. That basis of knowledge lends significant support to the tip's reliability." The Court noted that in this respect, the case contrasted with *Florida v. J. L.*, 529 U.S. 266 (2000), where the tip did not provide a basis to conclude that the tipster had actually seen the gun reportedly possessed by the defendant. It continued: "A driver's claim that another vehicle ran her off the road, however, necessarily implies that the informant knows the other car was driven dangerously." The Court noted evidence suggesting that the caller reported the incident soon after it occurred and stated, "That sort of contemporaneous report has long been treated as especially reliable." Again contrasting the case with *J.L.*, the Court noted that in *J.L.*, there was no indication that the tip was contemporaneous with the observation of criminal activity or made under the stress of excitement caused by a startling event. The Court determined that another indicator of veracity is the caller's use of the 911 system, which allows calls to be recorded and law enforcement to verify information about the caller. Thus, "a reasonable officer could conclude that a false tipster would think twice before using such a system . . . [and a] caller's use of the 911 system is therefore one of the relevant circumstances that, taken together, justified the officer's reliance on the information reported in the 911 call." But the Court cautioned, "None of this is to suggest that tips in 911 calls are *per se* reliable."

The Court noted that a reliable tip will justify an investigative stop only if it creates reasonable suspicion of criminal activity. It then determined that the caller's report of being run off the roadway created reasonable suspicion of an ongoing crime such as impaired driving. It stated:

> The 911 caller . . . reported more than a minor traffic infraction and more than a conclusory allegation of drunk or reckless driving. Instead, she alleged a specific and dangerous result of the driver's conduct: running another car off the highway. That conduct bears too great a resemblance to paradigmatic manifestations of drunk driving to be dismissed as an isolated example of recklessness. Running another vehicle off the road suggests lane positioning problems, decreased vigilance, impaired judgment, or some combination of those recognized drunk driving cues. . . . And the experience of many officers suggests that a driver who almost strikes a vehicle or another object—the exact scenario that ordinarily causes "running [another vehicle] off the roadway"—is likely intoxicated. . . . As a result, we cannot say that the officer acted unreasonably under these circumstances in stopping a driver whose alleged conduct was a significant indicator of drunk driving.

[*Author's note*: The Court's ruling raises questions about the continuing validity of prior North Carolina cases that had found insufficient evidence or reasonable suspicion based on an anonymous 911 caller, including *State v. Blankenship*, ___ N.C. App. ___, 748 S.E.2d 616 (2013); *State v. Peele*, 196 N.C. App. 668 (2009).

NORTH CAROLINA COURT OF APPEALS (page 96)

State v. Blankenship, ___ N.C. App. ___, 748 S.E.2d 616, 618 (2013). The court ruled that officers did not have reasonable suspicion to stop the defendant based on an anonymous tip from a taxicab driver. The taxicab driver anonymously contacted 911 by cell phone and reported that a red Mustang convertible with a black soft top, license plate XXT-9756, was driving erratically, running over traffic cones, and continuing west on a specified road. Although the 911 operator did not ask for the caller's name, the operator used the caller's cell phone number to later identify the taxicab driver as John Hutchby. The 911 call resulted in a "be on the lookout" being issued; minutes later officers spotted a red Mustang matching the caller's description, with "X" in the license plate, heading as indicated by the caller. Although the officers did not observe the defendant violating any traffic laws or see evidence of improper driving that would suggest impairment, the officers stopped the defendant. The defendant was charged with DWI. The court stated:

> [T]he officers did not have the opportunity to judge Hutchby's credibility firsthand or confirm whether the tip was reliable, because Hutchby had not been previously used and the officers did not meet him face-to-face. Since the officers did not have an opportunity to assess his credibility, Hutchby was an anonymous informant. Therefore, to justify a warrantless search and seizure, either the tip must have possessed sufficient indicia of reliability or the officers must have corroborated the tip.

The court found that neither requirement was satisfied.

[*Author's note*: The later ruling in *Navarette v. California*, 134 S. Ct. 1683 (2014) (anonymous caller's report provided reasonable suspicion for vehicle stop), summarized above, raises questions about the continuing validity of the *Blankenship* ruling.]

State v. Sutton, ___ N.C. App. ___, 754 S.E.2d 464, 468 (2014). The court ruled that an officer had reasonable suspicion to stop and frisk the defendant when the defendant was in a high crime area and made movements which the officer found suspicious. The defendant was in a public housing area patrolled by a Special Response Unit of the United States Marshals Service and the Drug Enforcement Administration concentrating on violent crimes and gun crimes. The officer in question had ten years of experience and was assigned to the Special Response Unit. Many people were banned from the public housing area—in fact, the banned list was nine pages long. On a prior occasion the officer heard shots fired near the area. In the present case, the officer saw the defendant walking normally while swinging his arms. When the defendant turned and "used his right hand to grab his waistband to clinch an item" after looking directly at the officer, the officer believed that the defendant was trying to hide something on his body. The officer then stopped the defendant to identify him, frisked him, and found a gun in the defendant's waistband.

State v. Knudsen, ___ N.C. App. ___, 747 S.E.2d 641 (2013). The court ruled that the trial court did not err by concluding that the seizure of the defendant by officers blocking the sidewalk on which he was walking was unsupported by reasonable suspicion. The officers observed the defendant walking down the sidewalk with a clear plastic cup in his hands filled with a clear liquid. The defendant entered his vehicle, remained in it for a period of time, and then exited his vehicle and began walking down the sidewalk, where he was stopped. The officers stopped and questioned the defendant because he was walking on the sidewalk with the cup and the officers wanted to know what was in the cup.

State v. Harwood, ___ N.C. App. ___, 727 S.E.2d 891 (2012). The court ruled that reasonable suspicion did not support the seizure of the defendant made as a result of an anonymous tip. When evaluating an anonymous tip in this context, the court must determine whether the tip taken as a whole possessed sufficient indicia of reliability. If not, the court must assess whether the anonymous tip could be made sufficiently reliable by independent corroboration. The tip at issue reported that the defendant would be selling marijuana at a certain location on a certain day and would be driving a white vehicle. The court ruled that given the limited details contained in the tip and the officers' failure to corroborate its allegations of illegal activity, the tip lacked sufficient indicia of reliability.

State v. Watkins, ___ N.C. App. ___, 725 S.E.2d 400 (2012). The court ruled that officers had reasonable suspicion to stop the defendant's vehicle. Officers had received an anonymous tip that a vehicle containing "a large amount of pills and drugs" would be traveling from Georgia through Macon County and possibly Graham County; the vehicle was described as a small- or mid-sized passenger car, maroon or purple in color, with Georgia license plates. Officers set up surveillance along the most likely route. When a small purple car passed the officers, they pulled out behind it. The car then made an abrupt lane change without signaling and slowed down by approximately 5–10 m.p.h. The officers ran the vehicle's license plate and discovered that the vehicle was registered to a person known to have outstanding arrest warrants. Although the officers were fairly certain that the driver was not the wanted person, they were unable to identify the passenger. They also saw the driver repeatedly looking in his rearview mirror and glancing over his shoulder. They then pulled the vehicle over. The court concluded that the defendant's lane change, combined with the anonymous tip and the defendant's other activities, were sufficient to give an experienced law enforcement officer reasonable suspicion that some illegal activity was taking place. Those other activities included the defendant's slow speed in the passing lane, frequent glances in his rearview mirrors, repeated glances over his shoulder, and driving a car registered to another person. Moreover, noted the court, not only was the defendant not the owner of the vehicle, but the owner was known to have outstanding arrest warrants. It was reasonable to conclude that the unidentified passenger may have been the vehicle's owner.

State v. Hemphill, ___ N.C. App. ___, 723 S.E.2d 142 (2012). The court ruled that an officer had reasonable suspicion that criminal activity was occurring to make an investigative stop of the defendant. At 10:10 p.m. the officer learned of a report of suspicious activity involving two men at used car lot Auto America. When the officer arrived at the scene he saw the defendant, who generally matched the description of one of the individuals reported, peering from behind a parked van. When the defendant spotted the officer, he ran, ignoring the officer's instructions to stop. After a 1/8-mile chase, the officer found the defendant trying to hide behind a dumpster.

State v. Brown, 217 N.C. App. 566 (2011). The court of appeals ruled that the trial court erred by denying the defendant's motion to suppress evidence of his alleged impairment when the evidence was the fruit of an illegal stop. An officer who was surveying an area in the hope of locating robbery suspects saw the defendant pull off to the side of a highway in a wooded area. The officer heard yelling and car doors slamming. Shortly thereafter, the defendant accelerated rapidly past the officer, but not to a speed warranting a traffic violation. Thinking that the defendant may have been picking up the robbery suspects, the officer followed the defendant for almost a mile. Although he observed no traffic violations, the officer pulled over the defendant's vehicle. The officer did not have any information regarding the direction in which the suspects fled, nor did he have a description of the getaway vehicle. The officer's reason for pulling over the defendant's vehicle was insufficient evidence of reasonable suspicion to support an investigative stop.

State v. Ellison, 213 N.C. App. 300 (2011), *aff'd on other grounds,* 366 N.C. 439 (2013). The court ruled that an officer had reasonable suspicion to stop the defendant's vehicle. An informant told the officer that after having his prescriptions for hydrocodone and Xanax filled, a man named Shaw would immediately take the medications to defendant Treadway's residence, where he sold the medications to Treadway. Treadway then sold some or all of the medications to defendant Ellison. The officer later learned that Shaw had prescriptions for Lorcet and Xanax, observed Shaw fill the prescriptions, and followed Shaw from the pharmacy to Treadway's residence. The officer watched Shaw enter and leave Treadway's residence. Minutes later the officer observed Ellison arrive. In stopping Ellison's vehicle, the officer also considered activities derived from surveillance at his place of work, which were consistent with drug-related activities. Although the officer had not had contact with the informant before this incident, one of his co-workers had worked with the informant and found the informant to be reliable—specifically, the informant previously provided information that resulted in arrests.

State v. Brown, 213 N.C. App. 617 (2011). The court ruled that officers had reasonable suspicion to stop the defendant. When officers on a gang patrol noticed activity at a particular house, they parked their car to observe. The area was known for criminal activity. The defendant exited from the rear of the house and approached the officers' car. One of the officers had previously made drug arrests in front of this house. As the defendant approached, one officer feared for his safety and got out of the car to have a better defensive position. When the defendant realized that the individuals were police officers, his "demeanor changed" and he appeared very nervous: he started to sweat, began stuttering, and would not speak loudly. Additionally, it was late and there was little light for the officers to see the defendant's actions.

In re A.J. M-B, 212 N.C. App. 586, 591, 592 (2011). The court of appeals ruled that the trial court erred by denying the juvenile's motion to dismiss a charge of resisting a public officer when reasonable suspicion did not support a stop of the juvenile for criminal activity. An anonymous caller reported to law enforcement that "two juveniles in Charlie district . . . [were] walking, supposedly with a shotgun or a rifle" in "an open field behind a residence." A dispatcher relayed the information to an officer, who went to an open field behind the residence. The officer saw two juveniles "pop their heads out of the wood line" and look at him. Neither was carrying a firearm. When the officer called out for them to stop, they ran around the residence and down the road.

State v. White, 214 N.C. App. 471 (2011). The court of appeals ruled that the trial court erred by denying the defendant's motion to suppress evidence obtained from an unlawful stop. Officers responded to a complaint of loud music in a location they regarded as a high crime area. The officers did not see the defendant engaged in any suspicious activity, nor did they observe any device capable of producing loud music. Rather, the defendant was merely standing outside at night, with two or three other men. These facts did not provide reasonable suspicion to justify an investigatory stop of the defendant. Thus, the officer's encounter with the defendant was entirely consensual; the defendant was free to ignore the interaction by running away, which he did. Once the officer caught up with the defendant and handcuffed him for resisting arrest, a seizure occurred. However, because the defendant's flight from the consensual encounter did not constitute resisting, the arrest was improper.

DWI Stops (page 108)
NORTH CAROLINA SUPREME COURT (page 108)

State v. Verkerk, ___ N.C. ___, 758 S.E.2d 387 (2014), *rev'g* ___ N.C. App. ___, 747 S.E.2d 658 (2013). In a DWI case where the defendant was initially stopped by a firefighter, the court determined that the trial court properly denied the defendant's motion to suppress that had challenged the firefighter's authority to make the initial stop. After observing the defendant's erratic driving and transmitting this information to the local police department, the firefighter stopped the defendant's vehicle. After some conversation, the defendant drove away. When police officers arrived on the scene, the firefighter indicated where the vehicle had gone. The officers located the defendant, investigated her condition, and charged her with DWI. On appeal, the defendant argued that because the firefighter had no authority to stop her, evidence from the first stop was improperly obtained. However, the court determined that it need not consider the extent of the firefighter's authority to conduct a traffic stop or even whether the defendant's encounter with him constituted a "legal stop." The court reasoned that the firefighter's observations of the defendant's driving, which were transmitted to the police before making the stop, established that the police officers had reasonable suspicion to stop the defendant. The court noted that this evidence was independent of any evidence derived from the firefighter's stop.

State v. Kochuk, 366 N.C. 549 (2013). The court, per curiam and without an opinion, reversed the decision of the North Carolina Court of Appeals, ___ N.C. App. ___, 741 S.E.2d 327 (2012), for the reasons stated in the dissenting opinion. An officer was on duty and traveling eastbound on Interstate 40, where there were three travel lanes. The officer was one to two car lengths behind the defendant's vehicle in the middle lane. The defendant momentarily crossed the right dotted line once while in the middle lane. He then made a legal lane change to the right lane and later drove on the fog line twice. The officer stopped the vehicle, and the defendant was later charged with DWI. The dissenting opinion stated that this case is controlled by *State v. Otto*, 366 N.C. 134 (2012), summarized immediately below. The defendant was weaving within his own lane, and the vehicle stop occurred at 1:10 a.m. These two facts coupled together, under *Otto*'s totality of the circumstances analysis, constituted reasonable suspicion for the DWI stop.

State v. Otto, 366 N.C. 134, 135 (2012), *rev'g* 217 N.C. App. 79 (2011). The court ruled that there was reasonable suspicion for a vehicle stop in this case. Around 11 p.m., an officer observed a vehicle drive past. The officer turned behind the vehicle and immediately noticed that it was weaving within its own lane. The vehicle never left its lane, but it was "constantly weaving from the center line to the fog line." The vehicle appeared to be traveling at the posted speed limit. After watching the vehicle weave in its own lane for about three-quarters of a mile, the officer stopped the vehicle. The defendant was issued a citation for impaired driving. The court of appeals determined that the traffic stop was unreasonable because it was supported solely by the defendant's weaving within her own lane. The supreme court disagreed, concluding that under the totality of the circumstances, there was reasonable suspicion for the traffic stop. The court noted that unlike other cases in which weaving within a lane was held insufficient to support reasonable suspicion, the weaving here was "constant and continual" over three-quarters of a mile. Additionally, the defendant was stopped around 11 p.m. on a Friday night.

NORTH CAROLINA COURT OF APPEALS (page 109)

State v. Weaver, ___ N.C. App. ___, 752 S.E.2d 240 (2013). The court ruled that the trial court, in granting the defendant's motion to suppress in a DWI case, erred by concluding that a licensed security guard was a state actor when he stopped the defendant's vehicle. In the alternative, the court ruled that even if the security guard was a state actor, reasonable suspicion supported the stop. The guard saw the defendant at 2:10 a.m. in rainy weather conditions, traveling approximately 25 m.p.h. in a 15 m.p.h. zone, and crossing over the center street lines several times. The time, poor weather conditions, speed, and failure to maintain lane control provided the guard with reasonable suspicion to stop the defendant.

State v. Derbyshire, ___ N.C. App. ___, 745 S.E.2d 886, 890, 893 (2013). The court ruled in this DWI case that the officer lacked reasonable suspicion to stop the defendant's vehicle. At 10:05 p.m. on a Wednesday night, an officer noticed that the defendant's high beams were on. The officer also observed the defendant weave once within his lane of travel. When pressed about whether the defendant weaved out of his lane, the officer indicated that "just . . . the right side of his tires" crossed over into the right-hand lane of traffic going in the same direction. The State presented no evidence that the stop occurred in an area of high alcohol consumption or that the officer considered such a fact as a part of her decision to stop the defendant. The court characterized the case as follows: "[W]e find that the totality of the circumstances . . . present one instance of weaving, in which the right side of Defendant's tires crossed into the right-hand lane, as well as two conceivable 'plus' factors—the fact that Defendant was driving at 10:05 on a Wednesday evening and the fact that [the officer] believed Defendant's bright lights were on before she initiated the stop." The court first noted that the weaving in this case was not constant and continuous. It then concluded that driving at 10:05 p.m. on a Wednesday evening and the officer's belief that the defendant's bright lights were on "are not sufficiently uncommon to constitute valid 'plus' factors" to justify the stop under a "weaving plus" analysis.

State v. Fields, ___ N.C. App. ___, ___, 723 S.E.2d 777, 779 (2012). The court ruled that an officer had reasonable suspicion to stop the defendant's vehicle when the defendant's weaving in his own lane was sufficiently frequent and erratic to prompt evasive maneuvers from other drivers. Distinguishing cases holding that weaving within a lane, standing alone, is insufficient to support a stop, the court noted that here "the trial court did not find only that defendant was weaving in his lane, but rather that defendant's driving was 'like a ball bouncing in a small room'" and that "[t]he driving was so erratic that the officer observed other drivers—in heavy traffic—taking evasive maneuvers to avoid defendant's car." The court determined that none of the other cases involved the level of erratic driving and potential danger to other drivers that was involved in this case.

Non-DWI Traffic Stops (page 112)
NORTH CAROLINA SUPREME COURT (page 112)

State v. Griffin, 366 N.C. 473, 477 (2013). The court ruled that the defendant's act of stopping his vehicle in the middle of the roadway and turning away from a license checkpoint supported reasonable suspicion for a vehicle stop. The trial court denied the defendant's motion to suppress, finding the stop constitutional. In an unpublished opinion, the court of appeals reversed on grounds that the checkpoint was unconstitutional. That court did not, however, comment on whether reasonable suspicion for the stop existed. The state supreme court allowed the State's petition for discretionary review to determine whether there was reasonable suspicion to initiate a stop of the defendant's vehicle and reversed. It reasoned:

Defendant approached a checkpoint marked with blue flashing lights. Once the patrol car lights became visible, defendant stopped in the middle of the road, even though he was not at an intersection, and appeared to attempt a three-point turn by beginning to turn left and continuing onto the shoulder. From the checkpoint [the officer] observed defendant's actions and suspected defendant was attempting to evade the checkpoint. . . . It is clear that this Court and the Fourth Circuit have held that even a legal turn, when viewed in the totality of the circumstances, may give rise to reasonable suspicion. Given the place and manner of defendant's turn in conjunction with his proximity to the checkpoint, we hold there was reasonable suspicion that defendant was violating the law; thus, the stop was constitutional. Therefore, because the [officer] had sufficient grounds to stop defendant's vehicle based on reasonable suspicion, it is unnecessary for this Court to address the constitutionality of the driver's license checkpoint.

State v. Heien, 366 N.C. 271 (2012), *cert. granted,* 134 S. Ct. 1872 (2014). The court reversed *State v. Heien,* ___ N.C. App. ___, 714 S.E.2d 827 (2011), and ruled that there was reasonable suspicion for a stop that led to the defendant's drug trafficking convictions. An officer stopped a vehicle based on a non-functioning brake light. The evidence indicated that although the left brake light was operating, the right light was not. Interpreting various statutes, the court of appeals had ruled that a vehicle is not required to have more than one operating brake light. It concluded that because the law had not been violated, the stop was unreasonable. Before the state supreme court, the State did not appeal the court of appeals' interpretation of statutory law. Instead, the State appealed only the court's determination that the stop was unreasonable. Thus, the issue before the court was whether an officer's mistake of law may nonetheless give rise to reasonable suspicion to conduct a routine traffic stop. On this issue the court ruled that an officer's objectively reasonable but mistaken belief that a traffic violation has occurred can provide reasonable suspicion for a stop. Applying this standard to the facts in this case, the court found that the officer's mistake was objectively reasonable and that the stop was justified. [As noted in the citation to this case, the United States Supreme Court has granted the defendant's petition for certiorari to review the ruling in this case. The Court will likely issue its ruling between late 2014 and June 2015.]

State v. Burke, 365 N.C. 415 (2012). In a per curiam ruling without a written opinion, the state supreme court affirmed the decision in *State v. Burke,* 212 N.C. App. 654, 658 (2011), in which the court of appeals ruled that the trial judge erred by denying the defendant's motion to suppress because reasonable suspicion did not support a stop of the defendant's vehicle. The officer stopped the vehicle because the numbers on its thirty-day tag looked "low," and the low number led him to "wonder[] about the possibility of the tag being fictitious." The court of appeals noted that it had previously ruled that thirty-day tags that were unreadable, concealed, obstructed, or illegible justified stops of the vehicles involved. In this case, however, although the officer testified that the thirty-day tag was dirty and worn, he was able to read the tag without difficulty. The tag was not faded. The information was clearly visible and was accurate and proper.

NORTH CAROLINA COURT OF APPEALS (page 114)

State v. Coleman, ___ N.C. App. ___, ___, ___, 743 S.E.2d 62, 65, 67 (2013). The court ruled that an officer lacked reasonable suspicion to stop the defendant's vehicle. A "be on the lookout" call was issued after a citizen caller reported that there was a cup of beer in a gold Toyota sedan with license number VST-8773 parked at the Kangaroo gas station at the corner of Wake Forest Road and Ronald Drive. Although the complainant wished to remain anonymous, the communications center obtained the caller's name as Kim Creech. An officer responded and observed a vehicle fitting the caller's description. The officer followed the driver as he pulled out of the lot and onto Wake Forest Road and then pulled him over. The officer did not observe any traffic violations. After a test indicated impairment, the defendant was charged with DWI. Noting that the officer's sole reason for the stop was Creech's tip, the court found that the tip was not reliable in its assertion of illegality because possessing an open container of alcohol in a parking lot is not illegal because the law applies only to highways, not public vehicular areas. It concluded: "Accordingly, Ms. Creech's tip contained no actual allegation of criminal activity." It further found that the officer's mistaken belief that the tip included an actual allegation of illegal activity was not objectively reasonable. Finally, the court concluded that even if the officer's mistaken belief was reasonable, it still would find the tip insufficiently reliable. Considering anonymous tip cases, the court ruled that although Creech's tip provided the license plate number and location of the car, "she did not identify or describe defendant, did not provide any way for [the] Officer . . . to assess her credibility, failed to explain her basis of knowledge, and did not include any information concerning defendant's future actions."

State v. Hernandez, ___ N.C. App. ___, 742 S.E.2d 825 (2013). The court ruled, relying on *State v. Hess,* 185 N.C. App. 530 (2007), that an investigative stop of the defendant's vehicle was lawful. Officers stopped the defendant's vehicle because it was registered in her name, her license was suspended, and they were unable to determine the driver's identity.

State v. Royster, ___ N.C. App. ___, ___, 737 S.E.2d 400, 406 (2012). (1) The court ruled that an officer had reasonable suspicion to stop the defendant's vehicle for speeding. The court rejected the defendant's argument that because the officer only observed the vehicle for three to five seconds, the officer did not have a reasonable opportunity to judge the vehicle's speed. The court noted that after his initial observation of the vehicle, the officer made a U-turn and began pursuing it. He testified that during his pursuit, the defendant "maintained his speed." Although the officer did not testify to a specific distance he observed the defendant travel, "some distance was implied" by his testimony concerning his pursuit of the defendant. Also, although it is not necessary that an officer have specialized training to be able to visually estimate a vehicle's speed, the officer in this case had specialized training in visual speed estimation. (2) The court rejected the defendant's argument that the officer lacked reasonable suspicion to stop his vehicle for speeding because there was insufficient evidence identifying the defendant as the driver. Specifically, the defendant noted that the officer lost sight of the vehicle for a short period of time. The officer only lost sight of the defendant for approximately thirty seconds, and when he saw the vehicle again, he recognized both the car and the driver. [*Author's note*: On this point the opinion discussed the court's earlier opinion in *State v. Lindsey,* ___ N.C. App. ___, 725 S.E.2d 350 (2012), which was later reversed by the North Carolina Supreme Court (see 366 N.C. 325 (2012)) four days before *Royster* was decided but not in time to be included in *Royster.* However, because the court distinguished *Lindsey,* its discussion of the reversed decision does not appear to undermine the ultimate ruling.]

State v. Canty, ___ N.C. App. ___, ___, ___, 736 S.E.2d 532, 536, 537 (2012). The court ruled that reasonable suspicion did not support a traffic stop. The State had argued that reasonable suspicion existed based on the driver's alleged crossing of the fog line on Interstate 40, the driver's and passenger's alleged nervousness and failure to make eye contact with officers as they drove by and alongside the patrol car, and the vehicle's slowed speed. The court found that the evidence failed to show that the vehicle crossed the fog line and, in the absence of a traffic violation, the officers' beliefs about the conduct of the driver and passenger were nothing more than an "unparticularized suspicion or hunch." It noted that nervousness, slowing down, and not making eye contact are not unusual reactions when passing law enforcement officers. The court also found it "hard to believe" that the officers could tell that the driver and passenger were nervous as they passed the officers on the highway and as the officers momentarily rode alongside the vehicle. The court also found the reduction in speed—from 65 m.p.h. to 59 m.p.h.—insignificant.

State v. Osterhoudt, ___ N.C. App. ___, 731 S.E.2d 454 (2012). The court ruled that an officer had reasonable suspicion to stop the defendant's vehicle based on observed traffic violations despite the officer's mistaken belief that the defendant also had violated G.S. 20-146(a) (drive on right side of highway). The officer's testimony that he initiated the stop after observing the defendant drive over the double yellow line was sufficient to establish a violation of G.S. 20-146(d)(1) (drive within single lane), (d)(3) (failure to obey direction of official traffic-control device regarding designated lanes), (d)(4) (failure to obey direction of official traffic-control device regarding changing lanes), and 20-153(a) (proper right turns at intersections). Therefore, regardless of his subjective belief that the defendant violated G.S. 20-146(a), the officer's testimony established objective criteria justifying the stop. The stop was reasonable, and the superior court erred in holding otherwise. The court noted that because the officer's reason for the stop was not based solely on his mistaken belief that the defendant violated G.S. 20-146(a) but, rather, was also because the defendant crossed the double yellow line, the case was distinguishable from others that had ruled that an officer's mistaken belief that a defendant had committed a traffic violation is not an objectively reasonable basis for a stop.

[*Author's note*: The ruling in *State v. McLamb,* 186 N.C. App. 124 (2007), discussed on page 115 and concerning mistake of law, may need to be reconsidered in light of the North Carolina Supreme Court ruling in *State v. Heien,* 366 N.C. 271 (2012), *cert. granted,* 134 S. Ct. 1872 (2004), discussed above. The continuing validity of *McLamb* is also dependent on how the United States Supreme Court rules in *Heien* after having granted certiorari to review it. Also, the ruling of *United States v. King*, 244 F.3d 736 (9th Cir. 2001), should be viewed with caution as to its applicability to North Carolina state courts in light of *Heien*.]

School Search and Seizure Cases (page 119)

In re T.A.S., 366 N.C. 269, 269 (2012). The state supreme court vacated and remanded the decision below, 213 N.C. App. 273 (2011) (holding that a search of a juvenile student's bra conducted by school officials and observed by a male law enforcement officer was constitutionally unreasonable), ordering further findings of fact. The court ordered the trial court to

> make additional findings of fact, including but not necessarily limited to: the names, occupations, genders, and involvement of all the individuals physically present at the "bra lift" search of T.A.S.; whether T.A.S. was advised before the search of the Academy's "no penalty" policy; and whether the "bra lift" search of T.A.S. qualified as a "more intrusive" search under the Academy's Safe School Plan.

The court further provided that "[i]f, after entry of an amended judgment or order by the trial court, either party enters notice of appeal, counsel are instructed to ensure that a copy of the Safe School Plan, discussed at the suppression hearing and apparently introduced into evidence, is included in the record on appeal."

Special Aspects of Stopping Authority (page 121)
Length of Time Allowed for an Investigative Stop (page 121)

State v. Velazquez-Perez, ___ N.C. App. ___, ___, 756 S.E.2d 869, 876 (2014). In a drug trafficking case, the court ruled that the trial court did not err by denying the defendant's motion to suppress drugs seized from a truck during a vehicle stop. The defendant argued that once the officer handed the driver a warning citation, the purpose of the stop was over and, accordingly, anything that occurred thereafter unconstitutionally prolonged the stop. The court noted that officers routinely check relevant documentation while conducting traffic stops. Here, although the officer had completed writing the warning citation, he had not completed his checks concerning the licenses, registration, insurance, travel logs, and invoices of the commercial vehicle. Thus, "The purpose of the stop was not completed until [the officer] finished a proper document check and returned the documents to [the driver and the passenger, who owned the truck]." The court noted that because the defendant did not argue the issue, it would not address which documents may be properly investigated during a routine commercial vehicle stop.

State v. Heien, ___ N.C. ___, 749 S.E.2d 278 (2013), *aff'g per curiam* ___ N.C. App. ___, 741 S.E.2d 1 (2013). [*Author's note*: Although this case is currently pending before the United States Supreme Court, with a ruling expected between late 2014 and June 2015, the case involves a different issue (reasonable mistake of law when making an investigative stop) than the ruling discussed in the text.] The state supreme court affirmed per curiam the ruling of the North Carolina Court of Appeals that had held that a valid traffic stop was not unduly prolonged and that, as a result, the defendant's consent to search his vehicle was valid. The stop was initiated at 7:55 a.m. and the defendant, a passenger who owned the vehicle, gave consent to search at 8:08 a.m. During this time, the two officers present discussed a malfunctioning vehicle brake light with the driver, discovered that the driver and the defendant claimed to be going to different destinations, and observed the defendant behaving unusually (he was lying down on the backseat under a blanket and remained in that position even when approached by one of the officers requesting his driver's license). After each person's name was checked for warrants, their licenses were returned. One officer then requested consent to search the vehicle. The officer's tone and manner were conversational and non-confrontational. No one was restrained, no guns were drawn, and neither person was searched before the request to search the vehicle was made. The supreme court ruled that the trial judge properly concluded that the defendant was aware that the purpose of the initial stop had been concluded and that further conversation between the officer and the defendant was consensual. The court also ruled that the defendant's consent to search the vehicle was valid even though the officer did not inform the defendant that he was searching for narcotics.

State v. Sellars, ___ N.C. App. ___, ___, 730 S.E.2d 208, 210 (2012). The court of appeals ruled that the trial court erred by granting the defendant's motion to suppress on the ground that officers impermissibly prolonged a lawful vehicle stop. Officers McKaughan and Jones stopped the defendant's vehicle after it twice weaved out of its lane. The officers had a drug dog with them. McKaughan immediately determined that the defendant was not impaired. Although the defendant's hand was shaking, he did not show extreme nervousness. McKaughan told the defendant that he would not get a citation but asked him to come to the police vehicle. While "casual conversation" ensued in the police car, Jones stood outside the defendant's vehicle. The defendant was polite, cooperative, and responsive. Upon entering the defendant's identifying information into his computer, McKaughan found an "alert" indicating that the defendant was a "drug dealer" and "known felon." He returned the defendant's driver's license and issued a warning ticket. While still in the police car, McKaughan asked the defendant if he had any drugs or weapons in his car. The defendant said no. After the defendant refused to give consent for a dog sniff of the vehicle, McKaughan had the dog conduct a sniff. The dog alerted to narcotics in the vehicle, and a search revealed a bag of cocaine. The period between the issuance of the warning ticket and the dog sniff was four minutes and thirty-seven seconds. Surveying two lines of cases from the court which "appear to reach contradictory conclusions" concerning whether a de minimis delay is unconstitutional, the court reconciled the cases and ruled that any prolonged detention of the defendant for conducting the drug dog sniff was de minimis and did not violate his rights.

State v. Lopez, ___ N.C. App. ___, ___, 723 S.E.2d 164, 169 (2012). The court ruled that reasonable suspicion supported the length of the stop in this case. Also, the officer's initial questions concerning the defendant's license, route of travel, and occupation were within the scope of the traffic stop. Any further detention was appropriate based on the following facts: The defendant did not have a valid driver's license. Although the defendant said he had just gotten off work at a construction job, he was well kept with clean hands and clothing. The defendant "became visibly nervous by breathing rapidly[;] . . . his heart appeared to be beating rapidly[;] he exchanged glances with his passenger and both individuals looked at an open plastic bag in the back seat of the vehicle." An officer saw dryer sheets protruding from an open bag containing a box of clear plastic wrap, which, due to his training and experience, the officer knew were used to package and conceal drugs. The defendant told the officer that the car he was driving belonged to a friend but that he was not sure of the friend's name.

Scope of an Investigative Stop (page 124)
NORTH CAROLINA SUPREME COURT (page 126)

State v. Williams, 366 N.C. 110, 117 (2012), *aff'g* 215 N.C. App. 1 (2011) (reasonable articulable suspicion justified extending traffic stop). The officer stopped the vehicle in which the defendant was a passenger for having illegally-tinted windows and issued a citation. The officer then asked for and was denied consent to search the vehicle. Thereafter he called for a canine trained in drug detection. When the dog arrived, it alerted on the car and drugs were found. Several factors supported the trial court's determination that reasonable suspicion supported extending the stop. First, the driver told the officer that she and the defendant passenger were coming from Houston, Texas, which was illogical given their direction of travel. Second, the defendant's inconsistent statement that they were coming from Kentucky and were traveling to Myrtle Beach "raise[d] a suspicion as to the truthfulness of the statements." Third, the driver's inability to tell the officer where they were going, along with her illogical answer about driving from Houston, permitted an inference that she "was being deliberately evasive, that she had been hired as a driver and intentionally kept uninformed, or that she had been coached as to her response if stopped." Fourth, the fact that the defendant initially suggested that she and the driver were cousins but then admitted that they just called each other cousins based on their long-term relationship, "could raise a suspicion that the alleged familial relationship was a prearranged fabrication." Finally, the vehicle, which had illegally-tinted windows, was owned by a third person. The state supreme court concluded:

> Viewed individually and in isolation, any of these facts might not support a reasonable suspicion of criminal activity. But viewed as a whole by a trained law enforcement officer who is familiar with drug trafficking and illegal activity on interstate highways, the responses were sufficient to provoke a reasonable articulable suspicion that criminal activity was afoot and to justify extending the detention until a canine unit arrived.

State v. Fisher, ___ N.C. App. ___, ___, 725 S.E.2d 40, 44 (2012). The court of appeals ruled that the trial court erred by concluding that an officer lacked reasonable suspicion to detain the defendant beyond the scope of a routine traffic stop. The officer lawfully stopped the vehicle being driven by the defendant for a seatbelt violation but then extended the detention in order to wait for the arrival of a canine unit. The State argued that numerous factors established reasonable suspicion that the defendant was transporting contraband: an overwhelming odor of air freshener in the car; the defendant claimed to have made a five-hour round trip to go shopping but had not purchased anything; the defendant was nervous; the defendant had pending drug charges and was known as a distributor of marijuana and cocaine; the defendant was driving in a pack of cars; the car was registered to someone else; the defendant never asked why he had been stopped; the defendant was "eating on the go"; and a handprint indicated that something recently had been placed in the trunk. Although the officer did not know about the pending charges until after the canine unit was called, the court found this to be a relevant factor. It reasoned: "The extended detention of defendant is ongoing from the time of the traffic citation until the canine unit arrives and additional factors that present themselves during that time are relevant to why the detention continued until the canine unit arrived." Even discounting several of these factors that might be indicative of innocent behavior, the court found that other factors—nervousness, the smell of air freshener, inconsistency concerning travel plans, driving a car not registered to the defendant, and the pending charges—supported a finding that reasonable suspicion existed.

Using Weapons or Handcuffs (page 133)

State v. Carrouthers, 213 N.C. App. 384 (2011). The court ruled that an officer's act of handcuffing the defendant during a *Terry* stop was reasonable and did not transform the stop into an arrest. The officer observed what he believed to be a hand-to-hand drug transaction between the defendant and another individual; the defendant was sitting in the back seat of a car, with two other people up front. While frisking the defendant, the officer felt an item consistent with narcotics, corroborating his suspicion of drug activity. The officer then handcuffed the defendant and recovered crack cocaine from his pocket. The circumstances presented a possible threat of physical violence, given the connection between drugs and violence and the fact that the officer was outnumbered by the people in the car. *See also* State v. Thorpe, ___ N.C. App. ___, 754 S.E.2d 213 (2014) (handcuffing defendant was permissible during investigative stop when single officer was also dealing with another suspect).

When an Officer's Interaction with a Person Is a Seizure under the Fourth Amendment (page 134)

State v. Price, ___ N.C. App. ___, 757 S.E.2d 309 (2014). The court ruled that the trial court erred by granting the defendant's motion to suppress. A wildlife officer on patrol in a pine forest approached the defendant, who was dressed in full camouflage and carrying a hunting rifle, and asked to see his hunting license. After the defendant showed his license, the officer asked how he got to the location. He replied that his wife transported him there. The officer then asked him whether he was a convicted felon, and the defendant admitted that he was. The officer seized the weapon, and the defendant was later charged with being a felon in possession of a firearm. The court ruled that the defendant was neither seized under the Fourth Amendment nor in custody under *Miranda* when the officer asked about his criminal history, and therefore the trial court erred by granting the motion to suppress.

State v. Knudsen, ___ N.C. App. ___, 747 S.E.2d 641 (2013). The court ruled that the trial court did not err by determining that the defendant was seized by two officers while walking on a sidewalk. Although the officers did not use physical force to restrain the defendant, both were in uniform and had weapons. One officer blocked the sidewalk with his vehicle and another used his bicycle to block the defendant's pedestrian travel on the sidewalk.

State v. Harwood, ___ N.C. App. ___, 727 S.E.2d 891 (2012). The court ruled that the defendant was seized under the Fourth Amendment when officers parked directly behind his stopped vehicle, drew their firearms, and ordered him and his passenger to exit the vehicle. After the defendant got out of his vehicle, an officer put him on the ground and handcuffed him.

The Authority to Make an Investigative Stop or Take Other Action without Reasonable Suspicion (page 141)

Detaining People Present When a Search Warrant Is Executed or Is Being Sought (page 141)

Bailey v. United States, 133 S. Ct. 1031, 1041, 1042 (2013). The Court held that the ruling in *Michigan v. Summers,* 452 U.S. 692 (1981) (officers executing a search warrant may detain occupants on the premises while the search is conducted), does not justify the detention of occupants beyond the immediate vicinity of the premises covered by a search warrant. In this case, the defendant left the premises before the search began, and officers waited to detain him until he had driven about one mile away. The Court reasoned that none of the rationales supporting the *Summers* decision—officer safety, facilitating the completion of the search, and preventing flight—apply with the same or similar force to the detention of recent occupants beyond the immediate vicinity of the premises. It further concluded that "[a]ny of the individual interests is also insufficient, on its own, to justify an expansion of the rule in *Summers* to permit the detention of a former occupant, wherever he may be found away from the scene of the search." It stated: "The categorical authority to detain incident to the execution of a search warrant must be limited to the immediate vicinity of the premises to be searched." The Court continued, noting that *Summers* also relied on the limited intrusion on personal liberty involved with detaining occupants incident to the execution of a search warrant. It concluded that when officers arrest an individual away from his or her home, there is an additional level of intrusiveness. The Court declined to precisely define the term "immediate vicinity," leaving it to the lower courts to make this determination based on "the lawful limits of the premises, whether the occupant was within the line of sight of his dwelling, the ease of reentry from the occupant's location, and other relevant factors."

Conducting Impaired-Driving and Driver's License Checkpoints (page 141)

NORTH CAROLINA SUPREME COURT (page 142)

State v. Griffin, 366 N.C. 473, 477 (2013). The court ruled that the defendant's act of stopping his vehicle in the middle of the roadway and turning away from a license checkpoint supported reasonable suspicion for a vehicle stop. The trial court denied the defendant's motion to suppress, finding the stop constitutional. In an unpublished opinion, the court of appeals reversed on grounds that the checkpoint was unconstitutional. That court did not, however, comment on whether reasonable suspicion for the stop existed. The state supreme court allowed the State's petition for discretionary review to determine whether there was reasonable suspicion to initiate a stop of the defendant's vehicle and reversed. It reasoned:

> Defendant approached a checkpoint marked with blue flashing lights. Once the patrol car lights became visible, defendant stopped in the middle of the road, even though he was not at an intersection, and appeared to attempt a three-point turn by beginning to turn left and continuing onto the shoulder. From the checkpoint [the officer] observed defendant's actions and suspected defendant was attempting to evade the checkpoint.... It is clear that this Court and the Fourth Circuit have held that even a legal turn, when viewed in the totality of the circumstances, may give rise to reasonable suspicion. Given the place and manner of defendant's turn in conjunction with his proximity to the checkpoint, we hold there was reasonable suspicion that defendant was violating the law; thus, the stop was constitutional. Therefore, because the [officer] had sufficient grounds to stop defendant's vehicle based on reasonable suspicion, it is unnecessary for this Court to address the constitutionality of the driver's license checkpoint.

NORTH CAROLINA COURT OF APPEALS (page 143)

State v. White, ___ N.C. App. ___, 753 S.E.2d 698 (2014). The court ruled that the trial court did not err by granting the defendant's motion to suppress evidence obtained as a result of a vehicle checkpoint. Specifically, the trial court did not err by concluding that a lack of a written policy in full force and effect at the time of the defendant's stop at the checkpoint constituted a substantial violation of G.S. 20-16.3A (requiring a written policy providing guidelines for checkpoints). The court also rejected the State's argument that a substantial violation of G.S. 20-16.3A could not support suppression; the State had argued that evidence only can be suppressed if there is a constitutional violation or a substantial violation of G.S. Chapter 15A.

Stopping Vehicle under Community Caretaking Doctrine (new section after "Conducting Information-Seeking Checkpoints" on page 146)

State v. Smathers, ___ N.C. App. ___, ___, ___, 753 S.E.2d 380, 384, 386 (2014). In a case where the State conceded that the officer had neither probable cause nor reasonable suspicion to seize the defendant, the court decided an issue of first impression and ruled that the officer's seizure of the defendant by stopping her vehicle was justified by the community caretaking doctrine. The officer stopped the defendant to see if she and her vehicle were okay after he saw her hit an animal on a roadway. Her driving did not give rise to any suspicion of impairment. During the stop the officer determined that the defendant was impaired and arrested her for DWI. The court noted that in adopting the community caretaking exception, "we must apply a test that strikes a proper balance between the public's interest in having officers help citizens when needed and the individual's interest in being free from unreasonable governmental intrusion." It went on to adopt the following test for application of the doctrine:

> [T]he State has the burden of proving that: (1) a search or seizure within the meaning of the Fourth Amendment has occurred; (2) if so, that under the totality of the circumstances an objectively reasonable basis for a community caretaking function is shown; and (3) if so, that the public need or interest outweighs the intrusion upon the privacy of the individual.

The court applied the test and found that the stop at issue fell within the community caretaking doctrine.

The Authority to Arrest: Probable Cause (page 150)

Objective Standard in Determining Probable Cause, Reasonable Suspicion, or the Fact of Arrest (page 159)

State v. Osterhoudt, ___ N.C. App. ___, 731 S.E.2d 454 (2012). The court ruled that the officer had reasonable suspicion to stop the defendant's vehicle based on observed traffic violations despite the officer's mistaken belief that the defendant also had violated G.S. 20-146(a) (drive on right side of highway). The officer's testimony that he initiated the stop after observing the defendant drive over the double yellow line was sufficient to establish a violation of G.S. 20-146(d)(1) (drive within single lane), (d)(3) (failure to obey direction of official traffic-control device regarding designated lanes), (d)(4) (failure to obey direction of official traffic-control device regarding changing lanes), and 20-153(a) (proper right turns at intersections). Therefore, regardless of his subjective belief that the defendant violated G.S. 20-146(a), the officer's testimony established objective criteria justifying the stop. The stop was reasonable, and the superior court erred in holding otherwise. The court noted that because the officer's reason for the stop was not based solely on his mistaken belief that the defendant violated G.S. 20-146(a) but, rather, was also because the defendant crossed the double yellow line, the case was distinguishable from others that had ruled that an officer's mistaken belief that a defendant had committed a traffic violation is not an objectively reasonable basis for a stop.

The Arrest Procedure (page 162)

Use of Force (page 162)

Plumhoff v. Rickard, 134 S. Ct. 2012, 2022 (2014). The United States Supreme Court ruled that officers did not use excessive force in violation of the Fourth Amendment when using deadly force to end a high speed car chase. The chase ended when officers shot and killed the fleeing driver. The driver's daughter filed a civil rights action under Title 42, Section 1983 of the United States Code (hereinafter Section 1983), alleging that the officers used excessive force in terminating the chase in violation of the Fourth Amendment. Given the circumstances of the chase—among other things, speeds in excess of 100 m.p.h. when other cars were on the road—the Court found it "beyond serious dispute that [the driver's] flight posed a grave public safety risk, and . . . the police acted reasonably in using deadly force to end that risk." The Court rejected the respondent's contention that, even if the use of deadly force was permissible, the officers acted unreasonably in firing a total of fifteen shots, stating: "It stands to reason that, if police officers are justified in firing at a suspect in order to end a severe threat to public safety, the officers need not stop shooting until the threat has ended."

Chapter 3

Law of Search and Seizure

Chapter 3

Law of Search and Seizure

Observations and Actions That May Not Implicate Fourth Amendment Rights (page 174)

The book stated that the Fourth Amendment protects a reasonable expectation of privacy, explained how a court determines whether a person has a reasonable expectation of privacy, and noted that absent a finding of such privacy, the Fourth Amendment is not violated by an officer's actions. The United States Supreme Court decided two cases (*United States v. Jones*[1] and *Florida v. Jardines*[2]) since the book's publication that ruled that certain physical intrusions on a person's private property may constitute a Fourth Amendment violation. The physical intrusion theory, derived from common law trespass, is a ground for finding a Fourth Amendment violation that is sufficient by itself and independent from the theory of a reasonable expectation of privacy. Thus, there are now two theories providing a basis for Fourth Amendment protections that must be considered in cases when the facts may support one or both theories.

The Court in *Jones* ruled that the government's installation of a GPS tracking device on a vehicle and its use of that device to monitor the vehicle's movements on public streets constituted a "search" within the meaning of the Fourth Amendment. Officers who suspected that the defendant was involved in drug trafficking installed a GPS device without a valid search warrant on the undercarriage of a vehicle while it was parked in a public parking lot in Maryland. Over the next twenty-eight days, the government used the device to track the vehicle's movements and once had to replace the device's battery when the vehicle was parked in a different public lot in Maryland. By means of signals from multiple satellites, the device established the vehicle's location within 50 to 100 feet and communicated that location by cellular phone to a government computer. It relayed more than 2,000 pages of data over the four-week period. The defendant was charged with several drug offenses. He unsuccessfully sought to suppress the evidence obtained through the GPS device. Before the United States Supreme Court, the government argued that a warrant was not required for the GPS device. Concluding that the evidence should have been suppressed, the Court characterized the government's conduct as having "physically occupied private property for the purpose of obtaining information." So characterized, the Court had "no doubt that such a physical intrusion would have been considered a 'search' within the meaning of the Fourth Amendment when it was adopted."[3] The Court declined to address whether the defendant had a reasonable expectation of privacy in the undercarriage of his car and in the car's locations on the public roads, concluding that such an analysis was not required when the intrusion—as here—"encroached on a protected area."[4]

---

1. 132 S. Ct. 945 (2012).
2. 133 S. Ct. 1409 (2013).
3. *Jones*, 132 S. Ct. at 949.
4. *Id.* at 952.

The Court in *Jardines* ruled that officers' use of a drug-sniffing dog on a homeowner's porch to investigate the contents of the home was a "search" within the meaning of the Fourth Amendment. The Court's reasoning was based on the theory that the officers engaged in a physical intrusion of a constitutionally protected area. Applying that principle, the Court ruled:

> The officers were gathering information in an area belonging to [the defendant] and immediately surrounding his house—in the curtilage of the house, which we have held enjoys protection as part of the home itself. And they gathered that information by physically entering and occupying the area to engage in conduct not explicitly or implicitly permitted by the homeowner.[5]

The Court did not decide the case on a reasonable expectation of privacy analysis.

Abandoned Property and Garbage (page 175)
Garbage (page 176)
The physical intrusion theory of the Fourth Amendment, discussed above under "Observations and Actions That May Not Implicate Fourth Amendment Rights," must be considered when officers enter the curtilage of a home to retrieve garbage.

Areas Outside the Home: Curtilage and Open Fields (page 177)
The Curtilage (page 177)
See the discussion of the physical intrusion theory of the Fourth Amendment, discussed above under "Observations and Actions That May Not Implicate Fourth Amendment Rights"; that theory must be considered when officers enter the curtilage of a home.

In *State v. Pasour*,[6] the North Carolina Court of Appeals ruled that the trial court erred by denying the defendant's motion to suppress property seized in a warrantless search. Based on a tip, officers went to a specified address and knocked on the front and side doors. After getting no answer, two officers went to the back of the residence. In the backyard they found and seized marijuana plants. The officers were within the curtilage when they viewed the plants, there was no evidence indicating that the plants were visible from the front of the house or from the road, and a "no trespassing" sign was plainly visible on the side of the house. Even if the officers did not see the sign, it is evidence of the homeowner's intent that the side and back of the home were not open to the public. There was no evidence of a path or anything else to suggest a visitor's use of the rear door. Instead, all visitor traffic appeared to be kept to the front door, and traffic to the rear was discouraged by the posted sign. Further, there was no evidence indicating that the officers had reason to believe that knocking at the back door would produce a response after knocking multiple times at the front and side doors had not. The court concluded that on these facts, "there was no justification for the officers to enter [d]efendant's backyard and so their actions were violative of the Fourth Amendment."[7] For a comprehensive analysis of this case, see the blog post by School of Government faculty member Jeffrey B. Welty cited in the accompanying footnote.[8]

---

5. *Jardines*, 133 S. Ct. at 1414. The Court made clear, however, that it was not questioning the constitutionality of knock-and-talk, which occurs when an officer (without a drug dog) walks to the front door, knocks, and attempts to ask questions of the resident if he or she is willing to converse with the officer. Approaching a home and knocking is no more than any private person might do with a homeowner's implicit invitation.

6. ___ N.C. App. ___, 741 S.E.2d 323 (2012).

7. ___ N.C. App. at ___, 741 S.E.2d at 326–27.

8. Jeff Welty, *Going to the Back Door*, N.C. CRIM. L., UNC SCH. OF GOV'T BLOG (Oct. 22, 2012), http://nccriminallaw.sog.unc.edu/?p=3933.

Open Fields and Woods (page 178)

See the discussion of the physical intrusion theory of the Fourth Amendment, discussed above under "Observations and Actions That May Not Implicate Fourth Amendment Rights"; that theory must be considered when officers enter the curtilage of a home.

Common Entranceway to Residence (page 179)

For an analysis of the potential effect on "knock and talk" of the trespass theory of the Fourth Amendment as enunciated in the United States Supreme Court cases of *United States v. Jones*[9] and *Florida v. Jardines*,[10] see the blog post by School of Government faculty member Jeffrey B. Welty cited in the accompanying footnote.[11]

Plain View Sensory Perceptions (Observation, Smell, Sound, Touch, and Taste) (page 180)

Footnote 45 (page 180)

The North Carolina Court of Appeals in *State v. Alexander*, ___ N.C. App. ___, 755 S.E.2d 82 (2014), noted the ruling in *State v. Church*, 110 N.C. App. 569 (1993), that inadvertence is not an element of a lawful search under the plain view doctrine when a search warrant is not involved. The court mentioned that post-*Church* cases continue to articulate inadvertence as an element of the doctrine in non-search warrant situations. As noted in the text of this footnote, these cases are erroneously doing so.

Observation into a Car (page 182)

Footnote 56 (page 182)

Although the odor of marijuana allows a warrantless search of a vehicle, it does not necessarily allow the warrantless search of an occupant. *See* State v. Malunda, ___ N.C. App. ___, 749 S.E.2d 280 (2013) (odor of marijuana emanating from driver's side of vehicle and marijuana being discovered on driver's side did not allow warrantless search of vehicle passenger when all the circumstances in this case were considered).

Use of Special Devices or Animals (page 183)

GPS tracking devices (page 184)

To the extent that the discussion in the book on pages 184–86 about Fourth Amendment issues involved in installing and monitoring a GPS device is now inconsistent with *United States v. Jones*[12] and the physical intrusion theory of the Fourth Amendment, discussed above under "Observations and Actions That May Not Implicate Fourth Amendment Rights," it should be disregarded.

A comprehensive analysis about complying with *Jones* by School of Government faculty member Jeffrey B. Welty is available in the blog post cited in the accompanying footnote.[13] While the resolution of many aspects of the *Jones* ruling awaits future appellate cases, officers should consider the following conservative course of action to avoid constitutional violations, unless their agency's legal advisor provides different advice.[14]

Officers should assume that judicial authorization is required before installing and using a GPS tracking device, whether stick-on or hard-wired, unless there are exigent circumstances that would obviate the need for such authorization. And prior judicial authorization is necessary regardless of the length of the monitoring.

---

9. 132 S. Ct. 945 (2012).

10. 133 S. Ct. 1409 (2013).

11. Jeff Welty, *Does the Trespass Theory of the Fourth Amendment Limit the Scope of Knock and Talks?* N.C. Crim. L., UNC Sch. of Gov't Blog (Dec. 3, 2013), http://nccriminallaw.sog.unc.edu/?p=4554.

12. 132 S. Ct. 945 (2012).

13. Jeff Welty, *Advice to Officers After* Jones, N.C. Crim. L., UNC Sch. of Gov't Blog (Jan. 30, 2012), http://nccriminallaw.sog.unc.edu/?p=3250.

14. The following text substantively derives from the Welty blog post, *supra* note 13, although the post delves more deeply on some topics.

Judicial authorization can be secured either by a search warrant or a court order. As explained in the blog post referenced above, a court order issued by a superior court judge appears to be the better approach. The application for a court order should contain a factual statement, under oath, establishing probable cause to support the use of the tracking device. Although likely not legally required, it may be helpful to explain the need to use a tracking device instead of taking other actions, such as visual surveillance.

The court order should include a finding of probable cause and a statement authorizing the installation and monitoring of the tracking device, including the authorization to enter private property to install it, if necessary. The order probably should also:

- Set a time limit on monitoring, for example, thirty days unless extended in a later order. The relevant Federal Rule of Criminal Procedure[15] provides for a forty-five-day renewable period of monitoring.
- Address whether and how the subject is to be notified of the use of the device. For example, the order could provide for service of the order when the monitoring is completed. The federal rule provides for service within ten days of the completion of monitoring, unless the judge finds a reason to order otherwise.
- Require the officer to notify the issuing judge once installation and monitoring are complete. This would be similar to the return requirement for a search warrant.

It is not clear whether the authorization to use the tracking device would include the tracking of a suspect beyond North Carolina's borders, but it would appear to be permissible.

Dogs (page 186)

The United States Supreme Court decided two cases (*Florida v. Jardines*[16] and *Florida v. Harris*[17]) since the book was published. The *Jardines* case is discussed above under "Observations and Actions That May Not Implicate Fourth Amendment Rights."

The Court in *Harris* ruled that the dog sniff in the case provided probable cause to search a vehicle. The Court rejected the ruling of the Florida Supreme Court that would have required the prosecution to present, in every case, an exhaustive set of records, including a log of the dog's performance in the field, to establish the dog's reliability. The Court found this "demand inconsistent with the 'flexible, common-sense standard' of probable cause."[18] It instructed:

> In short, a probable-cause hearing focusing on a dog's alert should proceed much like any other. The court should allow the parties to make their best case, consistent with the usual rules of criminal procedure. And the court should then evaluate the proffered evidence to decide what all the circumstances demonstrate. If the State has produced proof from controlled settings that a dog performs reliably in detecting drugs, and the defendant has not contested that showing, then the court should find probable cause. If, in contrast, the defendant has challenged the State's case (by disputing the reliability of the dog overall or of a particular alert), then the court should weigh the competing evidence. In all events, the court should not prescribe, as the Florida Supreme Court did, an inflexible set of evidentiary requirements. The question—similar to every inquiry into probable cause—is whether all the facts surrounding a dog's alert, viewed through the lens of common sense, would make a reasonably prudent person think that a search would reveal contraband or evidence of a crime. A sniff is up to snuff when it meets that test.[19]

Applying that test to the drug dog's sniff in the case at hand, the Court found that it had been satisfied and ruled that there was probable cause to search the defendant's vehicle.[20]

---

15. Fed. R. Crim. P. 41(e)(2)(C).

16. 133 S. Ct. 1409 (2013).

17. 133 S. Ct. 1050 (2013).

18. *Id*. at 1053 (citations omitted).

19. *Id*. at 1058.

20. For an analysis of *Harris*, see Jeff Welty, *Supreme Court: Alert by a Trained or Certified Drug Dog Normally Provides Probable Cause*, N.C. Crim. L., UNC Sch. of Gov't Blog (Feb. 20, 2013), http://nccriminallaw.sog.unc.edu/?p=4111.

Wiretapping, Eavesdropping, Access to Stored Electronic Communications, and Related Issues (page 187)

Searching Cell Phone Incident to Arrest (page 189)

The United States Supreme Court in *Riley v. California*[21] ruled that the search incident to arrest exception to the search warrant requirement did not apply to a search of a cell phone.[22] The Court stated that searches incident to arrest generally are justified (a) to ensure that the arrestee does not have a weapon and (b) to prevent the arrestee from destroying evidence and that cell phone searches do not implicate those concerns. "[O]fficers remain free to examine the physical aspects of a phone to ensure that it will not be used as a weapon,"[23] but the data on the phone does not pose a risk of physical harm. And there is little risk that the data on a phone will be destroyed by the arrestee.

The government had argued that even seized phones could be locked or remotely wiped if not inspected immediately, but the Court found little reason to believe that these practices were prevalent or could be remedied by a search incident to arrest. Further, the risk of such practices can be managed by using Faraday bags (which block the radio waves that cell phones use to communicate) and other tools. Thus, the Court found little justification for allowing phones to be searched incident to arrest.

The Court also found a strong privacy interest militating against such warrantless searches. It noted that phones often contain vast quantities of data, making a search intrusive far beyond the mere fact of arrest itself and far beyond the level of intrusion associated with more traditional searches of pockets, wallets, and purses incident to arrest. Many phones can access data stored on remote servers, making a search extend beyond the immediate area of the arrestee. Emphasizing the need to establish a clear and workable rule, the Court therefore categorically exempted cell phones from the search incident to arrest doctrine.

How does the *Riley* ruling affect law enforcement practices beyond the need for a search warrant to search a cell phone incident to arrest?

First, the ruling clearly would apply to other data devices that a person possesses when arrested, such as tablets and laptops.

Second, if an officer has probable cause to believe that a cell phone or other data device contains evidence of a crime, the officer may warrantlessly seize the phone[24] but must apply for a search warrant to search it, either by physically appearing before a judicial official or by applying remotely through an audio and video transmission under G.S. 15A-245(a)(3).[25]

If there is evidence supporting a Fourth Amendment exception to the search warrant requirement, such as exigent circumstances or consent to search, then an officer may warrantlessly seize the cell phone and search it. However, the Court made clear that exigent circumstances are not satisfied based merely on the possibility of remote wiping of data, locking of a phone, or data encryption—absent evidence, for example, of an imminent remote wiping attempt. The Court stated that if officers seize a phone in an unlocked state, they may be able to disable a phone's automatic-lock feature to prevent the phone from locking and encrypting data. Exigent circumstances may exist if there is an immediate need to search a cell phone to stop a serious crime in progress, such as kidnapping, violent acts, possible detonation of a bomb, or an imminent threat to officers.

---

21. 134 S. Ct. 2473 (2014). Two separate cases were subsumed under this name, and both involved officers who examined electronic data on cell phones without a search warrant as a search incident to arrest.

The discussion of *Riley* in the text is substantially derived from Jeff Welty, *Supreme Court: Can't Search Cell Phones Incident to Arrest*, N.C. CRIM. L., UNC SCH. OF GOV'T BLOG (June 26, 2014), http://nccriminallaw.sog.unc.edu/?s=riley.

22. The North Carolina Supreme Court had previously permitted such a search. State v. Wilkerson, 363 N.C. 382 (2009).

23. 134 S. Ct. at 2485.

24. The Court clearly indicated that an arrestee's phone may be seized without a search warrant while an officer seeks a search warrant.

25. Officers need to check whether their respective counties have the capacity and approval to consider a search warrant application as set out in the statute cited in the text.

Consent to search is another exception to the search warrant requirement. To obtain consent to search, an officer should make clear to the suspect the scope of the proposed search because of the large and diverse amount of data that may be contained in a phone. For example, an officer seeking a broad search could ask for consent to conduct "a complete search of the phone," while a more narrow request could ask for consent to search the "list of recent calls" or other limited kind of data.

The Court's opinion suggests that data stored in "the cloud" is protected by the Fourth Amendment. One of its justifications as to why cell phone searches are more intrusive than searches of physical objects is a phone's possible connection to a remote server ("the cloud") that contains the phone's data. If this feature makes phone searches more intrusive, it may follow that the remote data is generally subject to a Fourth Amendment expectation of privacy. That may forecast a reconsideration in whole or in part of the third-party doctrine in cases such as *United States v. Miller,*[26] at least as it applies to privacy-sensitive information.

The issues of whether the *Riley* ruling applies to cases that were final when *Riley* was decided[27] and the application of the Fourth Amendment's exclusionary rule to officers' searches conducted before the *Riley* ruling are discussed in the blog posts cited in the accompanying footnote.[28]

Silent Video Surveillance (page 192)

An analysis of video surveillance cases before and after the GPS case of *United States v. Jones*[29] is provided in a blog post by School of Government faculty member Jeffrey B. Welty cited in the accompanying footnote.[30]

Access to Real-Time (Prospective) or Historical Cell-Site Information (page 195)

The book notes that the case law is evolving, but the view of most (but not all) courts is that a court order based on the federal standard, which is less than probable cause, is sufficient to obtain historical cell-site information. However, a federal appellate court[31] has recently ruled, in light of various Justices' views of the Fourth Amendment's reasonable expectation of privacy principle in the GPS case of *United States v. Jones,*[32] discussed on page 31 of this cumulative supplement, that the Fourth Amendment requires a search warrant or court order based on probable cause to obtain historical cell-site information. Although this federal appellate court's ruling is not binding on North Carolina state courts,[33] until the United States Supreme Court or North Carolina appellate courts decide this issue, cautious officers may want to obtain historical cell-site information by following the court's ruling or consulting with a legal advisor before proceeding without a search warrant or court order based on probable cause.

26. 425 U.S. 435 (1976) (depositor has no reasonable expectation of privacy in copies of checks and other bank records that are in bank's possession).

27. The date of the *Riley* ruling was June 25, 2014.

28. Jessica Smith, *Riley and Retroactivity*, N.C. CRIM. L., UNC SCH. OF GOV'T BLOG (July 29, 2014), http://nccriminallaw.sog.unc.edu/?p=4872; Jeff Welty, *Riley and Good Faith*, N.C. CRIM. L., UNC SCH. OF GOV'T BLOG (July 30, 2014), http://nccriminallaw.sog.unc.edu/?p=4873.

29. 132 S. Ct. 945 (2012).

30. Jeff Welty, *Video Surveillance Cameras*, N.C. CRIM. L., UNC SCH. OF GOV'T BLOG (Dec. 12, 2013), http://nccriminallaw.sog.unc.edu/?p=4570.

31. United States v. Davis, 754 F.3d 1205 (11th Cir. 2014). Although the court distinguished two prior federal appellate rulings, its ruling appears to conflict with them, particularly with the Fifth Circuit's ruling, *In re Application of United States for Historical Cell Site Data*, 724 F.3d 600 (5th Cir. 2013) (federal law's lesser "specific and articulable facts" standard for court order for historical cell-site information, rather than Fourth Amendment's probable cause standard, is not per se unconstitutional); *see also In re* Application of U.S. for Order Directing Provider of Elec. Commc'n Serv. to Disclose Records to the Gov't, 620 F.3d 304 (3d Cir. 2010) (federal law's "specific and articulable facts" standard for court order for historical cell-site information is sufficient to issue court order, but court has discretion to require search warrant).

32. 132 S. Ct. 945 (2012).

33. State courts are required to follow rulings on federal constitutional issues if issued by the United States Supreme Court, but not if issued by lower federal appellate or district courts. In addition, because the federal circuit deciding *Davis* does not have jurisdiction over North Carolina federal courts, its ruling also does not automatically apply in those courts. However, the ruling may have persuasive force when North Carolina appellate courts or other federal appellate and district courts decide the issue.

Search and Seizure by Valid Consent (page 199)
People Who Are Entitled to Give Valid Consent (page 199)

The United States Supreme Court in *Fernandez v. California*[34] clarified an issue left open in *Georgia v. Randolph*[35] (discussed in the book on page 199): the validity of a consent search by a residential occupant after a co-occupant had previously objected to a search but is no longer physically present when the occupant consents. Officers in *Fernandez* saw a man apparently involved in a robbery run into a building. They heard screams and fighting coming from an apartment therein. A woman responded to a knock on the door. She had fresh injuries and admitted she had been in a fight. Fernandez, a co-occupant, then appeared at the door and objected to officers entering the apartment. Believing that Fernandez had assaulted the woman, the officers arrested him and took him to the police station. An hour later an officer returned to the apartment and obtained the woman's consent to search the apartment. The Court noted that *Randolph* had stressed that its ruling was limited to situations when an objecting occupant was physically present when the co-occupant consented to the search (in which case, officers cannot rely on that consent to enter). The Court ruled that as long as officers have an objectively reasonable basis to remove the defendant (that is, the officers' subjective motive for removal is irrelevant), the co-occupant's later consent is sufficient. In this case, the officers properly removed Fernandez so that they could speak with the alleged assault victim outside of Fernandez's intimidating presence. Also, there was probable cause to arrest Fernandez for assault.

With an objecting occupant's physical presence given prominence in *Fernandez*, it remains to be seen how physical presence will be defined in future cases. Does the objecting occupant need to be present exactly where the co-occupant is consenting, or is it sufficient if he or she is somewhere on or near the premises? The Court appeared to indicate that on or near the premises may be sufficient.[36] But the Court did not definitively decide the issue, and a future Court may decide it differently.

When officers are unsure of their authority to search pursuant to one occupant's consent when another occupant is objecting, they may wish to consult with their agency's legal advisor or obtain a search warrant if probable cause exists to search the premises. Or sometimes there will be other legal grounds to enter premises without consent or a search warrant, such as when there is an immediate need to protect a victim from harm, seize weapons for self-protection, make a protective sweep of the premises, etc.

Invasion of Privacy by a Search or Seizure with Sufficient Reason (page 207)
Search and Seizure of Evidence with Probable Cause (page 208)
Search of a Person for Evidence with Probable Cause (page 218)
Obtaining a blood sample when an impaired driver refuses a chemical test (page 219)

The statement in the text that "because the person's blood alcohol content will likely change while officers apply for a search warrant, exigent circumstances would exist in most cases to permit taking a blood sample without a search warrant," must be revised based on the United States Supreme Court ruling in *Missouri v. McNeely*.[37] The Court ruled that in impaired driving investigations, the natural dissipation of alcohol in the bloodstream does not constitute an exigency in every case sufficient to justify conducting a blood test without a search warrant. The Court noted that under *Schmerber v. California*[38] and the Court's case law, applying the exigent circumstances exception requires consideration of all of the facts and circumstances of the particular case. It then rejected the State's request for a per se rule

---

34. 134 S. Ct. 1126 (2014).

35. 547 U.S. 103 (2006).

36. The Court cited *Bailey v. United States*, 133 S. Ct. 1031 (2013) (detaining occupants of premises during search warrant execution is limited to immediate vicinity of premises to be searched).

37. 133 S. Ct. 1552 (2013).

38. 384 U.S. 757 (1966).

for blood testing in impaired driving cases, declining to "depart from careful case-by-case assessment of exigency."[39] It concluded that "while the natural dissipation of alcohol in the blood may support a finding of exigency in a specific case, as it did in *Schmerber*, it does not do so categorically. Whether a warrantless blood test of a drunk-driving suspect is reasonable must be determined case by case based on the totality of the circumstances."[40] For an analysis of *McNeely* by School of Government faculty member Shea R. Denning, see the blog post cited in the accompanying footnote.[41]

Search and Seizure to Protect Officers, Other People, or Property (page 222)

Search Incident to Arrest (page 223)

Scope of a search incident to the arrest of an occupant of a vehicle (page 225)

The end of the first paragraph of this section noted that *Arizona v. Gant* did not define *reasonable to believe*. The North Carolina Supreme Court in *State v. Mbacke*[42] ruled that the term paralleled the *reasonable suspicion* standard for an investigative stop.

Footnote 347 (page 226)

The North Carolina Supreme Court in *State v. Mbacke*[43] reversed the North Carolina Court of Appeals ruling cited in this footnote and ruled that a search of the defendant's vehicle incident to his arrest for carrying a concealed gun did not violate the Fourth Amendment under *Gant*. The court noted that it was not ruling that an arrest for carrying a concealed weapon always justified a search of a vehicle, but instead that the legality of the search would depend on the circumstances of each case, which in *Mbacke* included a report of the defendant's actions the prior night (shooting at a house) and his furtive behavior when officers confronted him.

Add the following case to this footnote: *State v. Watkins*, ___ N.C. App. ___, 725 S.E.2d 400 (2012) (search of vehicle driven by defendant was valid under *Gant* as incident to arrest of defendant's passenger for possession of drug paraphernalia).

Strip searches and body-cavity searches (page 226)

This section in the book discusses cases on strip searches and body-cavity searches. There have been three additional cases since the book was published, which are discussed below.

In *State v. Johnson*,[44] the North Carolina Court of Appeals ruled that probable cause and exigent circumstances supported an officer's roadside search of the defendant's underwear conducted after a vehicle stop and that the search was conducted in a reasonable manner. After finding nothing in the defendant's outer clothing, the officer placed the defendant on the side of his vehicle, with the vehicle between the defendant and the travelled portion of the highway. Other troopers stood around the defendant to prevent passers-by from seeing him. The officer pulled out the front waistband of the defendant's pants and looked inside. The defendant was wearing two pairs of underwear—an outer pair of boxer briefs and an inner pair of athletic compression shorts. Between the two pairs of underwear the officer found a cellophane package containing several smaller packages. There was probable cause to search when the defendant smelled of marijuana, officers found a scale of the type used to measure drugs in his car, a drug dog alerted in his car, and during a pat-down the officer noticed a blunt object in the inseam of the defendant's pants. Because narcotics can be easily and quickly hidden or destroyed, especially after a defendant has notice of an officer's intent to discover whether the defendant possessed them, such exigent circumstances may be sufficient to justify a warrantless search, as was the case here. In addition, the search here was conducted in a reasonable manner. Although the officer did not see the defendant's private parts, the level of the defendant's exposure was relevant in analyzing whether the search was

---

39. *McNeely*, 133 S. Ct. at 1554–55.

40. *Id.* at 1563. For a post-*McNeely* case finding exigent circumstances to take blood without a search warrant, see *State v. Dahlquist*, ___ N.C. App. ___, 752 S.E.2d 665 (2013), discussed in Shea Denning, *Four Hour Delay to Obtain Search Warrant an Exigency, At Least for Now*, N.C. Crim. L., UNC Sch. of Gov't Blog (Dec. 4, 2013), http://nccriminallaw.sog.unc.edu/?p=4556.

41. Shea Denning, *Supreme Court Weighs in on Nonconsensual, Warrantless Blood Draws in DWI Cases*, N.C. Crim. L., UNC Sch. of Gov't Blog (Apr. 18, 2013), http://nccriminallaw.sog.unc.edu/?p=4213.

42. 365 N.C. 403 (2012).

43. *Id.*

44. ___ N.C. App. ___, 737 S.E.2d 442 (2013).

reasonable. The court reasoned that the officer had a sufficient basis to believe that contraband was in the defendant's underwear, including the fact that although the defendant smelled of marijuana, a search of his outer clothing found nothing; the defendant turned away from the officer when the officer frisked his groin and thigh area; and the officer felt a blunt object in the defendant's crotch area during the pat-down. Finally, the court concluded that the officer took reasonable steps to protect the defendant's privacy when conducting the search.

In *State v. Fowler*,[45] the North Carolina Court of Appeals ruled that two roadside strip searches of the defendant were reasonable and constitutional. The court first rejected the State's argument that the searches were not strip searches. During both searches the defendant's private areas were observed by an officer, and during the second search the defendant's pants were removed and an officer searched inside of the defendant's underwear with his hand. Second, the court ruled that probable cause supported the searches. The officers stopped the defendant's vehicle for speeding after receiving information from another officer and his informant that the defendant would be traveling on a specified road in a silver Kia, carrying 3 grams of crack cocaine. The strip searches occurred after a consensual search of the defendant's vehicle produced marijuana but no cocaine. The court found competent evidence to show that the informant, who was known to the officers and had previously provided reliable information, provided sufficient reliable information, corroborated by an officer, to establish probable cause to believe that the defendant would be carrying a small amount of cocaine in his vehicle. When the consensual search of the defendant's vehicle did not produce the cocaine, the officers had sufficient probable cause, under the totality of the circumstances, to believe that the defendant was hiding the drugs on his person. Third, the court found that exigent circumstances supported the searches. Specifically, the officer knew that the defendant had prior experience with jail intake procedures and that he could reasonably expect that the defendant would attempt to get rid of evidence in order to prevent his going to jail. Fourth, the court found that the searches were reasonable. The trial court had determined that although the searches were intrusive, the most intrusive one occurred in a dark area away from the traveled roadway, with no one other than the defendant and the officers in the immediate vicinity. In addition, the trial court found that the officer did not pull down the defendant's underwear or otherwise expose his bare buttocks or genitals, and no females were present or within view during the search. The court determined that these findings supported the trial court's conclusion that, although the searches were intrusive, they were conducted in a discreet manner, away from the view of others, and were limited in scope to finding a small amount of cocaine based on the corroborated tip of a known, reliable informant.

In *State v. Robinson*,[46] the North Carolina Court of Appeals ruled that an officer had probable cause to arrest the defendant after he felt something hard between the defendant's buttocks during a weapons frisk. The officer properly inferred that the defendant might be hiding drugs in his buttocks. The officer knew that the defendant was sitting in a car parked in a high crime area, a large machete was seen in the car, and a passenger possessed what appeared to be cocaine. When officers began to speak with the vehicle's occupants, the defendant dropped a large sum of cash on the floor and made a quick movement behind his back. The court also ruled that the searching officer took reasonable steps to protect the defendant's privacy during an intrusive search that discovered a clear plastic baggie of crack cocaine located between the defendant's buttocks. The officer shielded the defendant from public view by opening his patrol car's rear door and stood directly behind the defendant. The patrol car's lights were not turned on. The shining of the officer's flashlight into the defendant's pants was the only illumination in the immediate vicinity, and there were no other people in the search area.

Inventory of an Arrestee's Possessions before the Arrestee Enters a Detention Facility (page 229)
Footnote 366 (page 229)
Add the following case to footnote 366: In *Florence v. Board of Chosen Freeholders*, 132 S. Ct. 1510 (2012), the United States Supreme Court ruled that reasonable suspicion is not required for a close visual inspection of arrestees who will be held in the general population of a detention facility. The Court rejected the assertion that certain detainees, such

---

45. ___ N.C. App. ___, 725 S.E.2d 624 (2012).
46. ___ N.C. App. ___, 727 S.E.2d 712 (2012). There was a dissenting opinion in this case, but the defendant later withdrew his appeal to the North Carolina Supreme Court, 366 N.C. 247 (2012).

as those arrested for minor offenses, should be exempt from this process unless they give officers a particular reason to suspect them of hiding contraband.

Entry or Search of a Home to Render Emergency Assistance or for Self-Protection (page 232)

Entering a home to seize weapons for self-protection (page 233)

In *Ryburn v. Huff*,[47] the United States Supreme Court reversed a federal appellate court's ruling that officers were not entitled to qualified immunity in a Section 1983 federal civil rights action that arose after the officers entered a home without a warrant. When officers responded to a call from a high school, the principal informed them that a student, Vincent Huff, was rumored to have written a letter threatening to "shoot up" the school. The officers learned that Vincent had been absent two days, that he was a victim of bullying, and that a classmate believed him to be capable of carrying out the alleged threat. Officers found these facts troubling in light of training suggesting that these characteristics are common among perpetrators of school shootings. When the officers went to Vincent's home and knocked at the door, no one answered. They then called the home phone and no one answered. When they called Vincent's mother's cell phone, she reported that she and Vincent were inside. Vincent and Mrs. Huff then came outside to talk with the officers. Mrs. Huff declined an officer's request to continue the discussion inside. When an officer asked Mrs. Huff if there were any guns in the house, she immediately turned around and ran inside. The officers followed and eventually determined the threat to be unfounded. The Huffs filed a Section 1983 action against the officers for violating their Fourth Amendment rights by entering their home without a search warrant. The federal district court ruled for the officers, concluding that they were entitled to qualified immunity because Mrs. Huff's odd behavior, combined with the information the officers gathered at the school, could have led reasonable officers to believe that there could be weapons inside the house and that the officers or others were in danger. A divided panel of a federal appellate court disagreed with the conclusion that the officers were entitled to qualified immunity. The United States Supreme Court reversed, determining that reasonable officers could have come to the conclusion that the Fourth Amendment permitted them to enter the residence if there was an objectively reasonable basis to fear that violence was imminent. The Court further determined that a reasonable officer could have come to such a conclusion based on the facts as found by the trial court.

---

47. 132 S. Ct. 987 (2012).

Chapter 3 Appendix: Case Summaries

Chapter 3 Appendix: Case Summaries

Search and Seizure Issues (page 247)

What Is a Search and Seizure and What Evidence May Be Searched for and Seized (page 247)

Definition of a Search (page 247)

Florida v. Jardines, 133 S. Ct. 1409, 1414 (2013). The Court ruled that officers' use of a drug-sniffing dog on a home-owner's porch to investigate the contents of the home is a "search" within the meaning of the Fourth Amendment. The Court's reasoning was based on the theory that the officers engaged in a physical intrusion of a constitutionally protected area. Applying that principle, the Court ruled:

> The officers were gathering information in an area belonging to [the defendant] and immediately surrounding his house—in the curtilage of the house, which we have held enjoys protection as part of the home itself. And they gathered that information by physically entering and occupying the area to engage in conduct not explicitly or implicitly permitted by the homeowner.

The Court did not decide the case on a reasonable expectation of privacy analysis.

United States v. Jones, 132 S. Ct. 945, 949, 952 (2012). The Court ruled that the government's installation of a GPS tracking device on a vehicle and its use of that device to monitor the vehicle's movements on public streets constituted a "search" within the meaning of the Fourth Amendment. Officers who suspected that the defendant was involved in drug trafficking installed a GPS device without a valid search warrant on the undercarriage of a vehicle while it was parked in a public parking lot in Maryland. Over the next twenty-eight days, the government used the device to track the vehicle's movements and once had to replace the device's battery when the vehicle was parked in a different public lot in Maryland. By means of signals from multiple satellites, the device established the vehicle's location within 50 to 100 feet and communicated that location by cellular phone to a government computer. It relayed more than 2,000 pages of data over the four-week period. The defendant was charged with several drug offenses. He unsuccessfully sought to suppress the evidence obtained through the GPS device. Before the United States Supreme Court the government argued that a warrant was not required for the GPS device. Concluding that the evidence should have been suppressed, the Court characterized the government's conduct as having "physically occupied private property for the purpose of obtaining information." So characterized, the Court had "no doubt that such a physical intrusion would have been considered a 'search' within the meaning of the Fourth Amendment when it was adopted." The Court declined to address whether the defendant had a reasonable expectation of privacy in the undercarriage of his car and in the car's locations on the public roads, concluding that such an analysis was not required when the intrusion—as here—"encroached on a protected area."

State v. Jones, ___ N.C. App. ___, 750 S.E.2d 883 (2013). The court ruled that the trial court did not err by requiring the defendant to enroll in lifetime satellite-based monitoring (SBM). The court rejected the defendant's argument that SBM was an unreasonable search and seizure under *United States v. Jones* (132 S. Ct. 945 (2012) (government's installation of a GPS tracking device on a vehicle and its use of that device to monitor the vehicle's movements on public streets constitutes a "search"). The court found *Jones* irrelevant to a civil SBM proceeding.

In re V.C.R., ___ N.C. App. ___, 742 S.E.2d 566 (2013). Although an officer had reasonable suspicion to stop a juvenile, the officer's subsequent conduct of ordering the juvenile to empty her pockets constituted a search, and this search was illegal; it was not incident to an arrest or consensual. The district court thus erred by denying the juvenile's motion to suppress.

State v. Chambers, 203 N.C. App. 373 (2010) (unpublished). The court ruled that a license tag displayed on the back of a vehicle, as required by North Carolina law, does not provide a defendant with a subjective or objective reasonable expectation of privacy in the license tag. Thus, an officer who ran the license tag through the Division of Criminal Information and the Division of Motor Vehicles for violations and warrants did not conduct a search under the Fourth Amendment.

Observations and Actions That May Not Implicate Fourth Amendment Rights (page 249)

Private Search or Seizure (page 249)

State v. Weaver, ___ N.C. App. ___, 752 S.E.2d 240 (2013). The court ruled that the trial court, in granting the defendant's motion to suppress in a DWI case, erred by concluding that a licensed security guard was a state actor when he stopped the defendant's vehicle. Determining whether a private citizen is a state actor requires consideration of the totality of the circumstances, with special consideration of (1) the citizen's motivation for the search or seizure; (2) the degree of governmental involvement, such as advice, encouragement, and knowledge about the nature of the citizen's activities; and (3) the legality of the conduct encouraged by the officer. Importantly, the court noted, once a private search or seizure has been completed, later involvement of government agents does not transform the original intrusion into a governmental search. Alternatively, the court ruled that even if the security guard was a state actor, reasonable suspicion existed for the stop.

Abandoned Property and Garbage (page 252)

NORTH CAROLINA COURT OF APPEALS (page 253)

State v. Joe, ___ N.C. App. ___, 730 S.E.2d 779 (2012). The court ruled that the defendant did not voluntarily abandon controlled substances. Noting that the defendant was illegally arrested without probable cause, the court concluded that property abandoned as a result of illegal police activity cannot be held to have been voluntarily abandoned.

Areas Outside the Home: Curtilage and Open Fields (page 255)

UNITED STATES SUPREME COURT (page 255)

Florida v. Jardines, 133 S. Ct. 1409, 1414 (2013). The Court ruled that officers' use of a drug-sniffing dog on a home-owner's porch to investigate the contents of the home is a "search" within the meaning of the Fourth Amendment. The Court's reasoning was based on the theory that the officers engaged in a physical intrusion of a constitutionally protected area. Applying that principle, the Court ruled:

> The officers were gathering information in an area belonging to [the defendant] and immediately surrounding his house—in the curtilage of the house, which we have held enjoys protection as part of the home itself. And they gathered that information by physically entering and occupying the area to engage in conduct not explicitly or implicitly permitted by the homeowner.

The Court did not decide the case on a reasonable expectation of privacy analysis. The concurring opinion concluded that the conduct was a search based on both property and reasonable expectation of privacy grounds.

NORTH CAROLINA COURT OF APPEALS (page 258)

State v. Malunda, ___ N.C. App. ___, 749 S.E.2d 280 (2013). The court ruled that the trial court erred by concluding that officers had probable cause to conduct a warrantless search of the defendant, a passenger in a stopped vehicle. After detecting an odor of marijuana on the driver's side of the vehicle, the officers conducted a warrantless search of the vehicle and discovered marijuana in the driver's side door. However, the officers did not detect an odor of marijuana on the vehicle's passenger side or on the defendant. The court found that none of the other circumstances, including the defendant's location in an area known for drug activity, his prior criminal history, his nervousness and failure to immediately produce identification, or his commission of the infraction of possessing an open container of alcohol in a motor vehicle, when considered separately or in combination, established probable cause to search the defendant's person.

State v. Grice, ___ N.C. App. ___, ___, 735 S.E.2d 354, 355 (2012), *review allowed,* ___ N.C. ___, 743 S.E.2d 179 (2013). The court ruled that a seizure of marijuana plants by officers was not justified under the plain view doctrine. Two officers went to the defendant's home on a tip that he was growing and selling marijuana; they parked behind a white car in the driveway. One of the officers walked up the driveway and knocked on the door; the other stayed in the driveway. While one officer was knocking on the door, the other looked "around the residence . . . from [his] point of view." Looking over the hood of the white car, he saw four plastic buckets about fifteen yards away. Plants were growing in three of the buckets that he immediately identified as marijuana. He pointed out the plants to the other officer, who also believed they were marijuana. The officers then walked to the backyard where the plants were growing beside an outbuilding and seized them. The court found that the plants were located within the curtilage. The court rejected the State's argument that the officers properly seized the marijuana plants because they were seen in plain view during a valid knock-and-talk. [*Author's note*: As noted in the citation to this case, the North Carolina Supreme Court granted the State's petition to review this ruling.]

State v. Pasour, ___ N.C. App. ___, ___, 741 S.E.2d 323, 326–27 (2012). The court of appeals ruled that the trial court erred by denying the defendant's motion to suppress property seized in a warrantless search. After receiving a tip that a person living at a specified address was growing marijuana, officers went to the address and knocked on the front and side doors. After getting no answer, two officers went to the back of the residence. In the backyard they found and seized marijuana plants. The officers were within the curtilage when they viewed the plants, there was no evidence indicating that the plants were visible from the front of the house or from the road, and a "no trespassing" sign was plainly visible on the side of the house. Even if the officers did not see the sign, it is evidence of the homeowner's intent that the side and back of the home were not open to the public. There was no evidence of a path or anything else to suggest a visitor's use of the rear door. Instead, all visitor traffic appeared to be kept to the front door, and traffic to the rear was discouraged by the posted sign. Further, there was no evidence indicating that the officers had reason to believe that knocking at the back door would produce a response after knocking multiple times at the front and side doors had not. The court concluded that on these facts, "there was no justification for the officers to enter [d]efendant's backyard and so their actions were violative of the Fourth Amendment."

State v. Ballance, ___ N.C. App. ___, 720 S.E.2d 856 (2012). The court of appeals ruled that the trial court did not err by rejecting the defendant's motion to suppress evidence obtained by officers when they entered the property in question. The court concluded that the property constituted an "open field," so that the investigating officers' entry onto the property and the observations made there did not constitute a "search" for Fourth Amendment purposes. The property consisted of 119 acres of wooded land used for hunting and did not contain any buildings or residences.

Plain View (Sensory Perception) (page 262)
NORTH CAROLINA COURT OF APPEALS (page 265)

State v. Grice, ___ N.C. App. ___, ___, 735 S.E.2d 354, 355 (2012), *review allowed,* ___ N.C. ___, 743 S.E.2d 179 (2013). The court ruled that a seizure of marijuana plants by officers was not justified under the plain view doctrine. Two officers went to the defendant's home on a tip that he was growing and selling marijuana; they parked behind a white car in the driveway. One of the officers walked up the driveway and knocked on the door; the other stayed in the driveway. While one officer was knocking on the door, the other looked "around the residence . . . from [his] point of view." Looking over the hood of the white car, he saw four plastic buckets about fifteen yards away. Plants were growing in three of the buckets that he immediately identified as marijuana. He pointed out the plants to the other officer, who also believed they were marijuana. The officers then walked to the backyard where the plants were growing beside an outbuilding and seized them. The court found that the plants were located within the curtilage. The court rejected the State's argument that the officers properly seized the marijuana plants because they were seen in plain view during a valid knock-and-talk. [*Author's note*: As noted in the citation to this case, the North Carolina Supreme Court granted the State's petition to review this ruling.]

Tracking Devices (page 272)

United States v. Jones, 132 S. Ct. 945, 949, 952 (2012). The Court ruled that the government's installation of a GPS tracking device on a vehicle and its use of that device to monitor the vehicle's movements on public streets constitute a "search" within the meaning of the Fourth Amendment. Officers who suspected that the defendant was involved in drug trafficking installed a GPS device without a valid search warrant on the undercarriage of a vehicle while it was parked in a public parking lot in Maryland. Over the next twenty-eight days, the government used the device to track the vehicle's movements and once had to replace the device's battery when the vehicle was parked in a different public lot in Maryland. By means of signals from multiple satellites, the device established the vehicle's location within 50 to 100 feet and communicated that location by cellular phone to a government computer. It relayed more than 2,000 pages of data over the four-week period. The defendant was charged with several drug offenses. He unsuccessfully sought to suppress the evidence obtained through the GPS device. Before the United States Supreme Court the government argued that a warrant was not required for the GPS device. Concluding that the evidence should have been suppressed, the Court characterized the government's conduct as having "physically occupied private property for the purpose of obtaining information." So characterized, the Court had "no doubt that such a physical intrusion would have been considered a 'search' within the meaning of the Fourth Amendment when it was adopted." The Court declined to address whether the defendant had a reasonable expectation of privacy in the undercarriage of his car and in the car's locations on the public roads, concluding that such an analysis was not required when the intrusion—as here—"encroached on a protected area."

Dogs (page 273)

Florida v. Harris, 133 S. Ct. 1050, 1053, 1058 (2013). The Court ruled that the dog sniff in this case provided probable cause to search a vehicle. The Court rejected the ruling of the Florida Supreme Court that would have required the prosecution to present, in every case, an exhaustive set of records, including a log of the dog's performance in the field, to establish the dog's reliability. The Court found this "demand inconsistent with the 'flexible, common-sense standard' of probable cause." It instructed:

> In short, a probable-cause hearing focusing on a dog's alert should proceed much like any other. The court should allow the parties to make their best case, consistent with the usual rules of criminal procedure. And the court should then evaluate the proffered evidence to decide what all the circumstances demonstrate. If the State has produced proof from controlled settings that a dog performs reliably in detecting drugs, and the defendant has not contested that showing, then the court should find probable cause. If, in contrast, the defendant has challenged the State's case (by disputing the reliability of the dog overall or of a particular alert), then the court should weigh the competing evidence. In all events, the court should not prescribe, as the Florida Supreme Court did, an inflexible set of evidentiary requirements. The question—similar to every inquiry into probable cause—is whether all the facts surrounding a dog's alert, viewed through the lens of common sense, would make a reasonably prudent person think that a search would reveal contraband or evidence of a crime. A sniff is up to snuff when it meets that test.

Applying that test to the drug dog's sniff in the case at hand, the Court found that it had been satisfied and ruled that there was probable cause to search the defendant's vehicle.

Florida v. Jardines, 133 S. Ct. 1409, 1414 (2013). The Court ruled that officers' use of a drug-sniffing dog on a homeowner's porch to investigate the contents of the home is a "search" within the meaning of the Fourth Amendment. The Court's reasoning was based on the theory that the officers engaged in a physical intrusion of a constitutionally protected area. Applying that principle, the Court ruled:

> The officers were gathering information in an area belonging to [the defendant] and immediately surrounding his house—in the curtilage of the house, which we have held enjoys protection as part of the home itself. And they gathered that information by physically entering and occupying the area to engage in conduct not explicitly or implicitly permitted by the homeowner.

The Court did not decide the case on a reasonable expectation of privacy analysis.

NORTH CAROLINA COURT OF APPEALS (page 274)

State v. Sellars, ___ N.C. App. ___, 730 S.E.2d 208 (2012). The court of appeals ruled that the trial court erred by granting the defendant's motion to suppress on the ground that officers impermissibly prolonged a lawful vehicle stop. Officers McKaughan and Jones stopped the defendant's vehicle after it twice weaved out of its lane. The officers had a drug dog with them. McKaughan immediately determined that the defendant was not impaired. Although the defendant's hand was shaking, he did not show extreme nervousness. McKaughan told the defendant that he would not get a citation but asked him to come to the police vehicle. While "casual conversation" ensued in the police car, Jones stood outside the defendant's vehicle. The defendant was polite, cooperative, and responsive. When entering the defendant's identifying information into his computer, McKaughan found an "alert" indicating that the defendant was a "drug dealer" and "known felon." He returned the defendant's driver's license and issued a warning ticket. While still in the police car, McKaughan asked the defendant if he had any drugs or weapons in his car. The defendant said no. After the defendant refused to give consent for a dog sniff of the vehicle, McKaughan had the dog do a sniff. The dog alerted to narcotics in the vehicle, and a search revealed a bag of cocaine. The time period between the issuance of the warning ticket and the dog sniff was four minutes and thirty-seven seconds. Surveying two lines of cases from the court which "appear to reach contradictory conclusions" on the question of whether a de minimis delay is unconstitutional, the court reconciled the cases and ruled that any prolonged detention of the defendant for the purpose of the drug dog sniff was de minimis and did not violate his rights.

State v. Smith, ___ N.C. App. ___, 729 S.E.2d 120 (2012). On what it described as an issue of first impression in North Carolina, the court ruled that a drug dog's positive alert at the front side driver's door of a motor vehicle is insufficient evidence to support probable cause to conduct a warrantless search of the person of a recent passenger of the vehicle who was standing outside the vehicle.

Search and Seizure by Valid Consent (page 279)
Voluntariness (page 279)
Generally (page 279)
NORTH CAROLINA COURT OF APPEALS (page 281)

State v. McMillan, 214 N.C. App. 320 (2011). The court ruled that the officers' advising the defendant that if he did not consent to giving oral swabs and surrendering certain items of clothing they would detain him until they obtained a search warrant did not negate the defendant's voluntary consent to the seizure of those items.

Officer's Statement about a Search Warrant (page 286)

State v. McMillan, 214 N.C. App. 320 (2011). The court ruled that the officers' advising the defendant that if he did not consent to giving oral swabs and surrendering certain items of clothing they would detain him until they obtained a search warrant did not negate the defendant's voluntary consent to the seizure of those items.

Scope of the Search (page 286)
NORTH CAROLINA COURT OF APPEALS (page 287)

State v. Lopez, ___ N.C. App. ___, 723 S.E.2d 164 (2012). The court ruled that the defendant's voluntary consent to a search of his vehicle extended to the officer's looking under the hood and in the vehicle's air filter compartment.

State v. Schiro, ___ N.C. App. ___, ___, 723 S.E.2d 134, 139 (2012). The court ruled that a consent search of the defendant's vehicle was not invalid because it involved taking off the vehicle's rear quarter panels. The trial court found that both rear quarter panels were fitted with a carpet/cardboard type interior trim and that they "were loose." Additionally, the trial court found that the officer "was easily able to pull back the carpet/cardboard type trim . . . covering the right rear quarter panel where he observed what appeared to be a sock with a pistol handle protruding from the sock."

Special Relationships (page 291)
Spouses and Other Shared Relationships (page 292)
UNITED STATES SUPREME COURT (page 292)

Fernandez v. California, 134 S. Ct. 1126 (2014). The Court in this case clarified an issue left open in *Georgia v. Randolph,* 547 U.S. 103 (2006) (discussed on page 199 of the book): the validity of a consent search by a residential occupant after a co-occupant has previously objected to a search but is no longer physically present when the occupant consents. Officers in *Fernandez* saw a man apparently involved in a robbery run into a building. They heard screams and fighting coming from an apartment therein. A woman responded to a knock on the door. She had fresh injuries and admitted that she had been in a fight. Fernandez, a co-occupant, then appeared at the door and objected to officers entering the apartment. Believing that Fernandez had assaulted the woman, the officers arrested him and took him to the police station. An hour later an officer returned to the apartment and obtained the woman's consent to search the apartment. The Court noted that *Randolph* had stressed that its ruling was limited to situations when an objecting occupant was physically present when the co-occupant consented to the search (in which case, officers cannot rely on that consent to enter). The Court ruled that as long as officers have an objectively reasonable basis to remove the defendant (that is, the officers' subjective motive for removal is irrelevant), the co-occupant's later consent is sufficient. In this case, the officers properly removed Fernandez so that they could speak with the alleged assault victim outside of Fernandez's intimidating presence. Also, there was probable cause to arrest Fernandez for assault. [*Author's note*: For additional analysis of this case, see page 35 of this cumulative supplement.]

Search and Seizure of Evidence with Probable Cause, Reasonable Suspicion, or Other Justification (page 298)
Vehicles, Including Containers within Vehicles (page 298)
Generally (page 298)
NORTH CAROLINA COURT OF APPEALS (page 301)

State v. Mitchell, ___ N.C. App. ___, 735 S.E.2d 438 (2012). The court ruled that the discovery of marijuana on a passenger provided probable cause to search a vehicle. After an officer stopped the defendant and determined that he had a revoked license, the officer told the defendant that the officer's K-9 dog would walk around the vehicle. At that point, the defendant indicated that his passenger had a marijuana cigarette, which she removed from her pants. The officer then searched the car and found marijuana in the trunk.

Strip Search of a Person (page 315)

State v. Johnson, ___ N.C. App. ___, 737 S.E.2d 442 (2013). The court ruled (1) that probable cause and exigent circumstances supported an officer's roadside search of the defendant's underwear conducted after a vehicle stop and (2) that the search was conducted in a reasonable manner. After finding nothing in the defendant's outer clothing, the officer placed the defendant on the side of his vehicle, with the vehicle between the defendant and the travelled portion of the highway. Other troopers stood around the defendant to prevent passers-by from seeing him. The officer pulled out the front waistband of the defendant's pants and looked inside. The defendant was wearing two pairs of underwear—an outer pair of boxer briefs and an inner pair of athletic compression shorts. Between the two pairs of underwear the officer found a cellophane package containing several smaller packages. There was probable cause to search when the defendant smelled of marijuana, officers found a scale of the type used to measure drugs in his car, a drug dog alerted in his car, and during a pat-down the officer noticed a blunt object in the inseam of the defendant's pants. Because narcotics can be easily and quickly hidden or destroyed, especially after a defendant has notice of an officer's intent to discover whether the defendant possessed them, such exigent circumstances may be sufficient to justify a warrantless search, as was the case here. In addition, the search here was conducted in a reasonable manner. Although the officer did not see the defendant's private parts, the level of the defendant's exposure was relevant to analyze whether the search was reasonable. The court reasoned that the officer had a sufficient basis to believe that contraband was in the defendant's underwear, including the fact that although the defendant smelled of marijuana, a search of his outer clothing found nothing; the defendant turned away from the officer when the officer frisked his groin and thigh area; and the officer felt a blunt object in the defendant's crotch area during the pat-down. Finally, the court concluded that the officer took reasonable steps to protect the defendant's privacy when conducting the search.

State v. Robinson, ___ N.C. App. ___, 727 S.E.2d 712 (2012). [*Author's note*: There was a dissenting opinion in this case, but the defendant later withdrew his appeal to the North Carolina Supreme Court, 366 N.C. 247 (2012).] The court ruled that an officer had probable cause to arrest the defendant after he felt something hard between the defendant's buttocks during a weapons frisk. The officer properly inferred that the defendant may be hiding drugs in his buttocks. The officer knew that the defendant was sitting in a car parked in a high crime area, a large machete was seen in the car, and a passenger possessed what appeared to be cocaine. When officers began to speak with the vehicle's occupants, the defendant dropped a large sum of cash on the floor and made a quick movement behind his back. The court also ruled that the searching officer had a sufficient basis to believe that the defendant had contraband beneath his underwear and that he took reasonable steps to protect the defendant's privacy during an intrusive search that discovered a clear plastic baggie of crack cocaine located between the defendant's buttocks. The officer shielded the defendant from public view by opening his patrol car's rear door and stood directly behind the defendant. The patrol car's lights were not turned on. The shining of the officer's flashlight into the defendant's pants was the only illumination in the immediate vicinity, and there were no other people in the search area. The officer did not put his hands or his flashlight down the defendant's pants.

State v. Fowler, ___ N.C. App. ___, 725 S.E.2d 624 (2012). The court ruled that two roadside strip searches of the defendant by officers were reasonable and constitutional. The court first rejected the State's argument that the searches were not strip searches. During both searches the defendant's private areas were observed by an officer, and during the second search the defendant's pants were removed and an officer searched inside of the defendant's underwear with his hand. Second, the court ruled that probable cause supported the searches. The officers stopped the defendant's vehicle for speeding after receiving information from another officer and his informant that the defendant would be traveling on a specified road in a silver Kia, carrying 3 grams of crack cocaine. The strip searches occurred after a consensual search of the defendant's vehicle produced marijuana but no cocaine. The court found competent evidence to show that the informant, who was known to the officers and had previously provided reliable information, provided sufficient reliable information, corroborated by an officer, to establish probable cause to believe that the defendant would be carrying a small amount of cocaine in his vehicle. When the consensual search of the defendant's vehicle did not produce the cocaine, the officers had sufficient probable cause, under the totality of the circumstances, to believe that the defendant was hiding the drugs on his person. Third, the court found that exigent circumstances supported the searches. Specifically, the officer knew that the defendant had prior experience with jail intake procedures and that he could reasonably expect that the defendant would attempt to get rid of evidence in order to prevent his going to jail. Fourth, the court found the searches were reasonable. The trial court had determined that although the searches were intrusive, the most intrusive one occurred in a dark area away from the traveled roadway, with no one other than the defendant and the officers in the immediate vicinity. In addition, the trial court found that the officer did not pull down the defendant's underwear or otherwise expose his bare buttocks or genitals, and no females were present or within view during the search. The court determined that these findings supported the trial court's conclusion that, although the searches were intrusive, they were conducted in a discreet manner, away from the view of others, and were limited in scope to finding a small amount of cocaine based on the corroborated tip of a known, reliable informant.

Search and Seizure of Evidence from a Person's Body (page 317)
UNITED STATES SUPREME COURT (page 317)

Maryland v. King, 133 S. Ct. 1958, 1970, 1977, 1978, 1980 (2013). The Court ruled that the defendant's Fourth Amendment rights were not violated by the taking of a DNA cheek swab as part of booking procedures. When the defendant was arrested in April 2009 for menacing a group of people with a shotgun and charged in state court with assault, he was processed for detention in custody at a central booking facility. Booking personnel used a cheek swab to take the DNA sample from him pursuant to the Maryland DNA Collection Act (Maryland Act). His DNA record was uploaded into the Maryland DNA database, and it was discovered that his profile matched a DNA sample from a 2003 unsolved rape case. He was later charged and convicted in the rape case. He challenged the conviction by arguing that the Maryland Act violated the Fourth Amendment. The Maryland appellate court agreed. The Supreme Court reversed. The Court found that using a buccal swab on the inner tissues of a person's cheek to obtain a DNA sample was a search. The Court noted that a determination of the reasonableness of the search requires a weighing of "the promotion of legitimate governmental interests" against "the degree to which [the search] intrudes upon an individual's privacy." It found that "[i]n the balance of reasonableness . . . , the Court must give great weight both to the significant government interest at stake in the identification of arrestees and to the unmatched potential of DNA identification to serve that interest." The Court noted in particular the superiority of DNA identification over fingerprint and photographic identification. Addressing privacy issues, the Court found that "the intrusion of a cheek swab to obtain a DNA sample is a minimal one." It noted that a gentle rub along the inside of the cheek does not break the skin and involves virtually no risk, trauma, or pain. And, distinguishing special needs searches, the Court noted: "Once an individual has been arrested on probable cause for a dangerous offense that may require detention before trial . . . his or her expectations of privacy and freedom from police scrutiny are reduced. DNA identification like that at issue here thus does not require consideration of any unique needs that would be required to justify searching the average citizen." The Court further determined that the processing of the defendant's DNA was not unconstitutional. The information obtained does not reveal genetic traits or private medical information, and testing is solely for the purpose of identification. Additionally, the Maryland Act protects against further invasions of privacy by, for example, limiting use to identification. The Court concluded:

> In light of the context of a valid arrest supported by probable cause respondent's expectations of privacy were not offended by the minor intrusion of a brief swab of his cheeks. By contrast, that same context of arrest gives rise to significant state interests in identifying respondent not only so that the proper name can be attached to his charges but also so that the criminal justice system can make informed decisions concerning pretrial custody. Upon these considerations the Court concludes that DNA identification of arrestees is a reasonable search that can be considered part of a routine booking procedure. When officers make an arrest supported by probable cause to hold for a serious offense and they bring the suspect to the station to be detained in custody, taking and analyzing a cheek swab of the arrestee's DNA is, like fingerprinting and photographing, a legitimate police booking procedure that is reasonable under the Fourth Amendment.

Missouri v. McNeely, 133 S. Ct. 1552, 1556, 1557, 1561, 1563 (2013). The Court ruled that in impaired driving investigations, the natural dissipation of alcohol in the bloodstream does not constitute an exigency in every case sufficient to justify conducting a blood test without a warrant. After stopping the defendant's vehicle for speeding and crossing the center line, an officer noticed several signs that the defendant was intoxicated, and the defendant acknowledged that he had consumed "a couple of beers." When the defendant performed poorly on field sobriety tests and declined to use a portable breath-test device, the officer placed him under arrest and began driving to the stationhouse. But when the defendant said that he would again refuse to provide a breath sample, the officer took him to a nearby hospital for blood testing. The officer did not attempt to secure a search warrant for the defendant's blood draw. Test results showed that the defendant's blood alcohol content was above the legal limit. The defendant was charged with impaired driving, and he moved to suppress the blood test. The trial court granted the defendant's motion, concluding that the exigency exception to the search warrant requirement did not apply because, apart from the fact that as in all intoxication cases, the defendant's blood alcohol was being metabolized by his liver, there were no circumstances suggesting that the officer faced an emergency in which he could not practicably obtain a search warrant. The state supreme court affirmed, reasoning that *Schmerber v. California*, 384 U.S. 757 (1966), required lower courts to consider the totality of the circumstances when determining whether exigency permits a nonconsensual, warrantless blood draw. The state court concluded that *Schmerber* "requires more than the mere dissipation of blood-alcohol evidence to support a warrantless blood draw in an alcohol-related case." (*See* State v. McNeely, 358 S.W.3d 65, 74 (2012).) The

United States Supreme Court affirmed. The Court noted that under *Schmerber* and the Court's case law, applying the exigent circumstances exception requires consideration of all of the facts and circumstances of the particular case. It then rejected the State's request for a per se rule for blood testing in impaired driving cases, declining to "depart from careful case-by-case assessment of exigency." It concluded: "[W]hile the natural dissipation of alcohol in the blood may support a finding of exigency in a specific case, as it did in *Schmerber*, it does not do so categorically. Whether a warrantless blood test of a drunk-driving suspect is reasonable must be determined case by case based on the totality of the circumstances."

State v. Dahlquist, ___ N.C. App. ___, 752 S.E.2d 665, 669 (2013). The court in this DWI case ruled that the trial court properly denied the defendant's motion to suppress evidence obtained from blood samples taken at a hospital without a search warrant when probable cause and exigent circumstances supported the warrantless blood draw. Noting the United States Supreme Court's ruling in *Missouri v. McNeely*, 133 S. Ct. 1552 (2013) (natural dissipation of alcohol in the bloodstream does not constitute an exigency in every case sufficient to justify conducting a blood test without a warrant), the court found that the totality of the circumstances supported the warrantless blood draw. Specifically, when the defendant pulled up to a checkpoint, an officer noticed the odor of alcohol and the defendant admitted to drinking five beers. After the defendant failed field sobriety tests, he refused to take an Intoxilyzer test. The officer then took the defendant to the hospital to have a blood sample taken without first obtaining a search warrant. The officer did this because it would have taken four to five hours to get the sample if he first had to travel to a magistrate for a warrant. The court noted however that the " 'video transmission' option that has been allowed by [G.S.] 15A-245(a)(3) [for communicating with a magistrate] . . . is a method that should be considered by arresting officers in cases such as this where the technology is available." It also advised: "[W]e believe the better practice in such cases might be for an arresting officer, where practical, to call the hospital and the [magistrate's office] to obtain information regarding the wait times on that specific night, rather than relying on previous experiences."

Wiretapping, Eavesdropping, and Video Surveillance (page 323)
UNITED STATES SUPREME COURT (page 323)

Riley v. California, 134 S. Ct. 2473, 2485 (2014). The Court ruled that the search incident to arrest exception to the search warrant requirement did not apply to a search of a cell phone. The Court stated that searches incident to arrest generally are justified (a) to ensure that the arrestee does not have a weapon and (b) to prevent the arrestee from destroying evidence and that cell phone searches do not implicate those concerns. "[O]fficers remain free to examine the physical aspects of a phone to ensure that it will not be used as a weapon," but the data on the phone does not pose a risk of physical harm. And there is little risk that the data on a phone will be destroyed by the arrestee.

The government had argued that even seized phones could be locked or remotely wiped if not inspected immediately, but the Court found little reason to believe that these practices were prevalent or could be remedied by a search incident to arrest. Further, the risk of such practices can be managed by using Faraday bags (which block the radio waves that cell phones use to communicate) and other tools. Thus, the Court found little justification for allowing phones to be searched incident to arrest.

The Court also found a strong privacy interest militating against such warrantless searches. It noted that phones often contain vast quantities of data, making a search intrusive far beyond the mere fact of arrest itself and far beyond the level of intrusion associated with more traditional searches of pockets, wallets, and purses incident to arrest. Many phones can access data stored on remote servers, making a search extend beyond the immediate area of the arrestee. Emphasizing the need to establish a clear and workable rule, the Court therefore categorically exempted cell phones from the search incident to arrest doctrine. [*Author's note*: For additional analysis of this case, see page 50 in this cumulative supplement.]

NORTH CAROLINA SUPREME COURT (page 324)

Delete the summary of *State v. Wilkerson*, 363 N.C. 382 (2009), on page 324. The *Wilkerson* ruling permitting a search of a cell phone incident to arrest has been effectively overruled by *Riley v. California*, 134 S. Ct. 2473 (2014).

Protective Searches (page 328)
Scope of Search Incident to Arrest (page 328)
Generally (page 328)
UNITED STATES SUPREME COURT (page 328)

Riley v. California, 134 S. Ct. 2473, 2485 (2014). The Court ruled that the search incident to arrest exception to the search warrant requirement did not apply to a search of a cell phone. The Court stated that searches incident to arrest generally are justified (a) to ensure that the arrestee does not have a weapon and (b) to prevent the arrestee from destroying evidence and that cell phone searches do not implicate those concerns. "[O]fficers remain free to examine the physical aspects of a phone to ensure that it will not be used as a weapon," but the data on the phone does not pose a risk of physical harm. And there is little risk that the data on a phone will be destroyed by the arrestee.

The government had argued that even seized phones could be locked or remotely wiped if not inspected immediately, but the Court found little reason to believe that these practices were prevalent or could be remedied by a search incident to arrest. Further, the risk of such practices can be managed by using Faraday bags (which block the radio waves that cell phones use to communicate) and other tools. Thus, the Court found little justification for allowing phones to be searched incident to arrest.

The Court also found a strong privacy interest militating against such warrantless searches. It noted that phones often contain vast quantities of data, making a search intrusive far beyond the mere fact of arrest itself and far beyond the level of intrusion associated with more traditional searches of pockets, wallets, and purses incident to arrest. Many phones can access data stored on remote servers, making a search extend beyond the immediate area of the arrestee. Emphasizing the need to establish a clear and workable rule, the Court therefore categorically exempted cell phones from the search incident to arrest doctrine. [*Author's note*: For additional analysis of this case, see page 49 in this cumulative supplement.]

Arrest of an Occupant of a Vehicle (page 331)

State v. Watkins, ___ N.C. App. ___, 725 S.E.2d 400 (2012). The court ruled that the search of a vehicle driven by the defendant was valid under *Gant* as incident to the arrest of the defendant's passenger for possession of drug paraphernalia. Officers had a reasonable belief that evidence relevant to the passenger's possession of drug paraphernalia might be found in the vehicle. Additionally, the objective circumstances provided the officers with probable cause for a warrantless search of the vehicle, including that drug paraphernalia was found on the passenger, there was an anonymous tip that the vehicle would be transporting drugs, there were outstanding arrest warrants for the car's owner, the defendant behaved nervously while driving and upon exiting the vehicle, and there was an alert by a drug-sniffing dog.

State v. Mbacke, 365 N.C. 403, 409, 409–10, 410, 411 (2012). The state supreme court reversed the court of appeals and determined that a search of the defendant's vehicle incident to his arrest for carrying a concealed gun did not violate the Fourth Amendment. The defendant was indicted for, among other things, trafficking in cocaine and carrying a concealed gun. Officers were dispatched to a specific street address in response to a 911 caller's report that a black male armed with a black handgun, wearing a yellow shirt, and driving a red Ford Escape was parked in his driveway and that the male had "shot up" his house the previous night. Officers Walley and Horsley arrived at the scene less than six minutes after the 911 call. They observed a black male (later identified as the defendant) wearing a yellow shirt and backing a red or maroon Ford Escape out of the driveway. The officers exited their vehicles, drew their weapons, and moved toward the defendant while ordering him to stop and put his hands in the air. Officer Woods then arrived and blocked the driveway to prevent escape. The defendant initially rested his hands on his steering wheel, but then lowered them towards his waist. Officers then began shouting at the defendant to keep his hands in sight and to exit his vehicle. The defendant raised his hands and stepped out of his car, kicking or bumping the driver's door shut as he did so. Officers ordered the defendant to lie on the ground and then handcuffed him, advising him that he was being detained because they had received a report that a person matching his description was carrying a weapon. After the defendant said that he had a gun in his waistband and officers found the gun, the defendant was arrested for carrying a concealed gun. The officers secured the defendant in the back of a patrol car, returned to his vehicle, and opened the driver's side door. Officer Horsley immediately saw a white brick wrapped in green plastic protruding from beneath the driver's seat. As Officer Horsley was showing this to Officer Walley, the defendant attempted to escape from the patrol car. After re-securing the defendant, the officers searched his vehicle incident to the arrest but found no other contraband. The white brick turned out to be 993.8 grams of cocaine. The court noted that the case required it to apply *Arizona v. Gant*, 556 U.S. 332 (2009) (officers may search a vehicle incident to arrest only if (1) the arrestee is unsecured and within reaching distance of the passenger compartment when the search is conducted or (2) it is reasonable to believe that evidence relevant to the crime of arrest might be found in the vehicle). It began its analysis by concluding that, as used in the second prong of the *Gant* test, the term "reasonable to believe" establishes a threshold lower than probable cause that "parallels the objective 'reasonable suspicion' standard sufficient to justify a *Terry* stop." Thus, it held that "when investigators have a reasonable and articulable basis to believe that evidence of the offense of arrest might be found in a suspect's vehicle after the occupants have been removed and secured, the investigators are permitted to conduct a search of that vehicle." Applying that standard, the court concluded:

[D]efendant was arrested for . . . carrying a concealed gun. The arrest was based upon defendant's disclosure that the weapon was under his shirt. Other circumstances . . . such as the report of defendant's actions the night before and defendant's furtive behavior when confronted by officers, support a finding that it was reasonable to believe additional evidence of the offense of arrest could be found in defendant's vehicle. Accordingly, the search was permissible under *Gant* . . . ."

The court concluded by noting that it "[was] not holding that an arrest for carrying a concealed weapon is *ipso facto* an occasion that justifies the search of a vehicle." It expressed the belief that "the 'reasonable to believe' standard required by *Gant* will not routinely be based on the nature or type of the offense of arrest and that the circumstances of each case ordinarily will determine the propriety of any vehicular searches conducted incident to an arrest."

Protective Sweep of Premises (page 333)

State v. Dial, ___ N.C. App. ___, ___, 744 S.E.2d 144, 146 (2013). The court of appeals ruled that the trial court did not err by denying the defendant's motion to suppress evidence discovered as a result of a protective sweep of his residence when officers had a reasonable belief based on specific and articulable facts that the residence harbored an individual who posed a danger to the officers' safety. Officers were at the defendant's residence to serve an order for arrest. Although the defendant on prior encounters had answered his door promptly, this time he did not respond for ten to fifteen minutes after an officer knocked and announced his presence. The officer heard shuffling on the other side of the front door. When two other officers arrived, the first officer briefed them on the situation, showed them the order for arrest, and explained his belief based on past experience that weapons were normally inside. When the deputies again approached the residence, "the front door flew open" and the defendant exited. The officers then issued verbal commands to the defendant, but he walked down the front steps with his hands raised, failing to comply with the officers' instructions. As soon as the first officer reached the defendant, the other officers entered the home and performed a protective sweep, lasting about thirty seconds. Evidence supporting the protective sweep included that the officers viewed the open door to the residence as a "fatal funnel" that could provide someone inside with a clear shot at the officers, the defendant's unusually long response time and resistance, the known potential threat of weapons inside the residence, shuffling noises that could have indicated more than one person inside the residence, the defendant's alarming exit from the residence, and the defendant's own actions that led him to be arrested in the open doorway.

Frisk (page 334)
Generally (page 334)
NORTH CAROLINA COURT OF APPEALS (page 336)

State v. Sutton, ___ N.C. App. ___, 754 S.E.2d 464 (2014). The court ruled that an officer had reasonable suspicion to stop and frisk the defendant when the defendant was in a high crime area and made movements which the officer found suspicious. The defendant was in a public housing area patrolled by a Special Response Unit of the United States Marshals Service and the Drug Enforcement Administration concentrating on violent crimes and gun crimes. The officer in question had ten years of experience and was assigned to the Special Response Unit. Many people were banned from the public housing area—in fact, the banned list was nine pages long. On a prior occasion the officer heard shots fired near the area. In the present case, the officer saw the defendant walking normally while swinging his arms. When the defendant turned and "used his right hand to grab his waistband to clinch an item" after looking directly at the officer, the officer believed that the defendant was trying to hide something on his body. The officer then stopped the defendant to identify him, frisked him, and found a gun in the defendant's waistband.

State v. Phifer, ___ N.C. App. ___, ___, 741 S.E.2d 446, 448, 449 (2013). The court ruled that the trial court improperly denied the defendant's motion to suppress. An officer saw the defendant walking in the middle of the street. The officer stopped the defendant to warn him about impeding the flow of street traffic. After issuing this warning, the officer frisked the defendant because of his "suspicious behavior," specifically, that he "appeared to be nervous and kept moving back and forth." The court found that "the nervous pacing of a suspect, temporarily detained by an officer to warn him not to walk in the street, is insufficient to warrant further detention and search."

State v. Hemphill, ___ N.C. App. ___, 723 S.E.2d 142 (2012). The court of appeals ruled that an officer, after feeling a screwdriver and wrench on the defendant's person during a pat-down, was justified in removing the tools because they both constituted a potential danger to the officer and were suggestive of criminal activity at a closed business late at night.

In re D.B., 214 N.C. App. 489 (2011). The court of appeals ruled that the trial court erred by admitting evidence obtained by an officer who exceeded the proper scope of a *Terry* frisk. After the officer stopped the juvenile, he conducted a weapons frisk and found nothing. When the officer asked the juvenile to identify himself, the juvenile did not respond. Because the officer thought he felt an identification card in the juvenile's pocket during the frisk, he retrieved it. It turned out to be a stolen credit card, which was admitted into evidence. Although officers who lawfully stop a person may ask a moderate number of questions to determine the person's identity and gain information confirming or dispelling their suspicions that prompted the stop, no authority suggests that an officer may physically search a person for evidence of his or her identity in connection with a *Terry* stop.

Plain Feel or Touch Doctrine (page 343)
NORTH CAROLINA COURT OF APPEALS (page 344)

State v. Reid, ___ N.C. App. ___, 735 S.E.2d 389, 391 (2012). The court ruled that a seizure of cocaine was justified under the "plain feel" doctrine. While searching the defendant, the officer "felt a large bulge" in his pocket and immediately knew based on its packing that it was narcotics.

State v. Richmond, 215 N.C. App. 475, 481, 482 (2011). An officer was present at a location to execute a search warrant in connection with drug offenses. The court of appeals ruled that evidence supported the trial court's finding that the officer, based on his training and experience, immediately formed the opinion during a pat-down that a bulge in the defendant's pants contained a controlled substance. Although the officer testified that he felt a "knot" in the defendant's pants that he could not "describe with any specificity," the officer also testified that he had discovered similar knots before in his six years of experience and had previously discovered "[b]ags of marijuana, bags of cocaine, bags of crack."

Entering Premises for Public Safety Reasons (page 350)

Ryburn v. Huff, 132 S. Ct. 987 (2012). The United States Supreme Court reversed a federal appellate court ruling that officers were not entitled to qualified immunity in a Section 1983 federal civil rights action that arose after the officers entered a home without a warrant. When officers responded to a call from a high school, the principal informed them that a student, Vincent Huff, was rumored to have written a letter threatening to "shoot up" the school. The officers learned that Vincent had been absent two days, that he was a victim of bullying, and that a classmate believed him to be capable of carrying out the alleged threat. Officers found these facts troubling in light of training suggesting that these characteristics are common among perpetrators of school shootings. When the officers went to Vincent's home and knocked at the door, no one answered. They then called the home phone and no one answered. When they called Vincent's mother's cell phone, she reported that she and Vincent were inside. Vincent and Mrs. Huff then came outside to talk with the officers. Mrs. Huff declined an officer's request to continue the discussion inside. When an officer asked

Mrs. Huff if there were any guns in the house, she immediately turned around and ran inside. The officers followed and eventually determined the threat to be unfounded. The Huffs filed a Section 1983 action against the officers for violating their Fourth Amendment rights by entering their home without a search warrant. The federal district court ruled for the officers, concluding that they were entitled to qualified immunity because Mrs. Huff's odd behavior, combined with the information the officers gathered at the school, could have led reasonable officers to believe that there could be weapons inside the house and that family members or the officers themselves were in danger. A divided panel of a federal appellate court disagreed with the conclusion that the officers were entitled to qualified immunity. The United States Supreme Court reversed, determining that reasonable officers could have come to the conclusion that the Fourth Amendment permitted them to enter the residence if there was an objectively reasonable basis to fear that violence was imminent. It further determined that a reasonable officer could have come to such a conclusion based on the facts as found by the trial court.

Search Warrants, Administrative Inspection Warrants, and Nontestimonial Identification Orders

Chapter 4

Search Warrants, Administrative Inspection Warrants, and Nontestimonial Identification Orders

Part I. Search Warrants (page 360)

Introduction (page 360)
Advantages of a Search Warrant (page 360)

Footnote 6 (page 360)

Add the following case summary to this footnote: Messerschmidt v. Millender, 132 S. Ct. 1235 (2012) (Court ruled that officer had qualified immunity in civil rights lawsuit against him because it was not entirely unreasonable to believe that he had probable cause to support issuance of search warrant for all firearms, firearm-related materials, and gang paraphernalia; the fact that the officer sought and obtained approval of the search warrant application from a superior law enforcement officer and a prosecutor provided further support for the conclusion that he could reasonably believe the search warrant was supported by probable cause).

Description of the Property to Be Seized (page 366)
Evidence in Computers (page 369)

Footnote 60 (page 369)

For an analysis of the application of the plain view theory when an officer searches a computer with a search warrant and encounters crimes other than those which are the object of the search warrant, see the blog post by School of Government faculty member Jeffrey B. Welty cited in the accompanying footnote.[1]

---

1. Jeff Welty, *Computer Searches and Plain View*, N.C. CRIM. L., UNC SCH. OF GOV'T BLOG (Nov. 21, 2013), http://nccriminallaw.sog.unc.edu/?p=4537.

Execution and Return of the Search Warrant (page 390)

People on the Premises (page 395)

Nonpublic Place (page 395)

Detaining and frisking (page 395)

In *Michigan v. Summers*,[2] the United States Supreme Court in 1981 upheld an officer's authority under the Fourth Amendment to detain—without reasonable suspicion or probable cause—people at a residence where a search warrant is being executed. The defendant in *Summers* was detained on a walkway leading down from the front steps of a house that was to be searched for drugs pursuant to a search warrant. The Court recognized three important interests, considered together, that justified the detention: (1) officer safety; (2) facilitating the completion of the search by preventing those inside from interfering with the officers; and (3) preventing flight if incriminating evidence was found.

The Court ruled in *Bailey v. United States*[3] that *Summers* did not authorize officers, who saw defendant Bailey leaving in a vehicle from the premises where a search warrant was about to be executed for a gun involved in a drug purchase, to delay making a detention until the defendant was about a mile away. The Court stated that the *Summers* ruling and its reasoning was limited to people in the immediate vicinity of the premises to be searched, which clearly did not include where Bailey was stopped. The Court reasoned that officer safety did not support the automatic detention of a person who was not in the immediate vicinity; officers have the authority to post officers near the premises to bar or detain anyone attempting to enter. If officers find that it would be dangerous to detain a departing person in front of the premises (possibly alerting anyone inside), they are not required to stop that person. Concerning facilitating the completion of the search, Bailey's presence a mile away was not a threat. If he had returned, officers could have clearly detained him. The need to prevent flight if incriminating evidence was found simply did not apply to Bailey, who was some distance from the premises. The Court concluded that Bailey's detention under the *Summers* ruling was not reasonable under the Fourth Amendment.

The Court declined to precisely define the term "immediate vicinity," leaving it to the lower courts to make this determination based on "the lawful limits of the premises, whether the occupant was within the line of sight of his dwelling, the ease of reentry from the occupant's location, and other relevant factors."[4]

The Court noted that if officers elect to defer a detention until a suspect or departing occupant of the premises leaves the immediate vicinity, the legality of a detention under the Fourth Amendment will be governed by other standards, such as those pertaining to investigative stops based on reasonable suspicion or arrests supported by probable cause. Factors to consider are (1) information already in the officers' possession before the search warrant was obtained; (2) any incriminating acts by the person leaving the premises, such as appearing to be armed or possessing the evidence being sought; and (3) any information communicated to the detaining officers from those conducting the search of the premises. The Court mentioned that the searching officers in *Bailey* had radioed the detaining officers of their discovery of guns and drugs in the premises, and this information may have provided probable cause to arrest.

As a result of *Bailey*, officers planning to execute a search warrant need to consider how to respond if they interact with people who are not within the immediate vicinity of the premises. If they detain or arrest someone not in the immediate vicinity, they must remember that reasonable suspicion or probable cause will be required.

Inventory of Seized Property (page 397)

Completing returns and inventories for computer search warrants is discussed in the blog post by School of Government faculty member Jeffrey B. Welty cited in the accompanying footnote.[5]

---

2. 452 U.S. 692 (1981).

3. 133 S. Ct. 1031 (2013).

4. *Id*. at 1042.

5. Jeff Welty, *Returns and Inventories for Computer Search Warrants*, N.C. CRIM. L., UNC SCH. OF GOV'T BLOG (Nov. 19, 2013), http://nccriminallaw.sog.unc.edu/?p=4534.

Return of the Search Warrant (page 397)

Completing returns and inventories for computer search warrants is discussed in the blog post by School of Government faculty member Jeffrey B. Welty cited in the accompanying footnote.[6]

Sealing Search Warrant from Public Inspection (page 397)

Footnote 200 (page 397)

An additional case for this footnote: *In re* Baker, ___ N.C. App. ___, 727 S.E.2d 316 (2012) (when search warrants were unsealed in accordance with procedures set forth in a senior resident superior court judge's administrative order, and when the State failed to make a timely motion to extend the period for which the documents were sealed, the trial judge did not err by unsealing the documents).

Disposition of Seized Property Pending Trial (page 397)

Whether officers may immediately destroy hazardous chemicals and other dangerous items (for example, methamphetamine laboratories) before a defendant has had a chance to examine and test them is discussed in the blog post by School of Government faculty member Jeffrey B. Welty cited in the accompanying footnote.[7]

Search Warrant Forms

Search Warrant Form AOC-CR-119 (page 407)

A revised search warrant form, dated June 2012, is available on the North Carolina Court System's website (www.nccourts.org/Forms/Documents/19.pdf). The revision added a block in which the magistrate may accept the return of the search warrant when the clerk's office is not open, and the magistrate agrees to forward the search warrant as soon as possible on the office's next business day.

Search Warrant Form AOC-CR-155 (page 409)

A revised form for a search warrant for blood or urine in DWI cases, dated April 2014, is available on the North Carolina Court System's website (www.nccourts.org/Forms/Documents/711.pdf). The revision added a block in which the magistrate may accept the return of the search warrant when the clerk's office is not open, and the magistrate agrees to forward the search warrant as soon as possible on the office's next business day.

---

6. *Id.*

7. Jeff Welty, *Search Warrants for Meth Labs*, N.C. Crim. L., UNC Sch. of Gov't Blog (Feb. 6, 2014), http://nccriminallaw.sog.unc.edu/?p=4625. The analysis is contained in a PDF file whose link is provided in the blog post.

Part II. Administrative Inspection Warrants (page 425)

Authority for Issuing Administrative Inspection Warrants (page 425)

Legislation enacted in 2011[8] placed limitations on periodic inspections by counties and cities of residential buildings and structures. Such an inspection may be conducted, with limited exceptions,[9] only when there is "reasonable cause," which in this case means when

- the landlord or owner has a history of more than two verified violations of the housing ordinances or codes within a twelve-month period;
- there has been a complaint that substandard conditions exist within the building or there has been a request that the building be inspected;
- the inspection department has actual knowledge of an unsafe condition within the building; or
- violations of local ordinances or codes are visible from the outside of the property.[10]

For an extensive analysis of this legislation, see the School of Government publication cited in the accompanying footnote.[11]

Issuing an Administrative Inspection Warrant (page 426)

Completing Warrant Forms (page 426)

Periodic Inspection Warrant (page 426)

See the discussion above of 2011 legislation that limited the use of periodic inspection warrants for residential buildings and structures.

Juveniles and Nontestimonial Identification Procedures (page 434)

Footnote 285 (page 434)

The correct statutory citations are G.S. 7B-2103 through -2109; 15A-502(c).

---

8. S.L. 2011-281, which amended G.S. 153A-364 (periodic inspections by counties) and 160A-424 (periodic inspections by cities).

9. Periodic inspections may be conducted in accordance with the state fire prevention code (or when otherwise required by state law) or as part of a targeted effort within a geographic area that has been designated by the county commissioners or city council.

10. G.S. 153A-364(a) (counties); 160A-424(a) (cities).

11. C. Tyler Mulligan, *Residential Rental Property Inspections, Permits, and Registration: Questions and Answers*, Community & Econ. Dev. Bull. No. 8 (UNC School of Government, Nov. 2011), http://sogpubs.unc.edu/electronicversions/pdfs/cedb8.pdf.

Chapter 4 Appendix: Case Summaries

Chapter 4 Appendix: Case Summaries

I. Search Warrants (page 445)

Probable Cause (page 445)
Generally (page 445)
NORTH CAROLINA COURT OF APPEALS (page 448)

State v. Rayfield, ___ N.C. App. ___, 752 S.E.2d 745, 753 (2014). The court in a child sex case ruled that the trial court did not err by denying the defendant's motion to suppress evidence obtained pursuant to a search warrant authorizing a search of his house. The victim told officers about various incidents occurring in several locations (the defendant's home, a motel, etc.) from the time that she was eight years old until she was eleven. The affidavit alleged that the defendant had shown the victim pornographic videos and images in his home. The affidavit noted that the defendant is a registered sex offender and requested a search warrant to search his home for magazines, videos, computers, cell phones, and thumb drives.

The court rejected the defendant's argument that the victim's information to the officers was stale, given the lengthy gap of time between when the defendant allegedly showed the victim the images and the actual search. It concluded: "Although [the victim] was generally unable to provide dates to the attesting officers . . . her allegations of inappropriate sexual touching by Defendant over a sustained period of time allowed the magistrate to reasonably conclude that probable cause was present to justify the search of Defendant's residence." It noted that "when items to be searched are not inherently incriminating [as here] and have enduring utility for the person to be searched, a reasonably prudent magistrate could conclude that the items can be found in the area to be searched." It concluded:

> There was no reason for the magistrate in this case to conclude that Defendant would have felt the need to dispose of the evidence sought even though acts associated with that evidence were committed years earlier. Indeed, a practical assessment of the information contained in the warrant would lead a reasonably prudent magistrate to conclude that the computers, cameras, accessories, and photographs were likely located in Defendant's home even though certain allegations made in the affidavit referred to acts committed years before.

State v. McKinney, ___ N.C. App. ___, 752 S.E.2d 726 (2014). The court ruled that the trial court erred by denying the defendant's suppression motion because the search warrant authorizing a search of the defendant's apartment was not supported by probable cause. The warrant application was based on the following evidence. An anonymous citizen reported observing suspected drug-related activity at and around the defendant's apartment. The officer then saw an individual named Foushee come to the apartment and leave after six minutes. Foushee was searched and arrested after he was found with marijuana and a large amount of cash. A search of Foushee's phone revealed text messages between Foushee and a person named Chad who proposed a drug transaction. The court acknowledged that this evidence established probable cause that Foushee had been involved in a recent drug transaction. However, it found the evidence insufficient to establish probable cause that there were illegal drugs at the defendant's apartment.

State v. Oates, ___ N.C. App. ___, 736 S.E.2d 228 (2012). Reversing the trial court, the court of appeals ruled that probable cause supported the issuance of a search warrant to search the defendant's residence. Although the affidavit supporting the warrant was based on information from anonymous callers, law enforcement corroborated specific information provided by a certain caller so that the tip had sufficient indicia of reliability. In addition, the affidavit provided a sufficient nexus between the items sought and the residence to be searched. Finally, the court ruled that the information was not stale.

Executing a Search Warrant (page 467)

People Present during the Execution of a Search Warrant (page 470)

Detaining People Present (page 470)

Bailey v. United States, 133 S. Ct. 1031, 1041, 1042 (2013). The United States Supreme Court ruled that *Michigan v. Summers,* 452 U.S. 692 (1981) (officers executing a search warrant may detain occupants on the premises while the search is conducted), does not justify the detention of occupants beyond the immediate vicinity of the premises covered by a search warrant. In this case, the defendant left the premises before the search began and officers waited to detain him until he had driven about one mile away. The Court reasoned that none of the rationales supporting the *Summers* decision—officer safety, facilitating the completion of the search, and preventing flight—apply with the same or similar force to the detention of recent occupants beyond the immediate vicinity of the premises. It further concluded that "[a]ny of the individual interests is also insufficient, on its own, to justify an expansion of the rule in *Summers* to permit the detention of a former occupant, wherever he may be found away from the scene of the search." It stated: "The categorical authority to detain incident to the execution of a search warrant must be limited to the immediate vicinity of the premises to be searched." The Court continued, noting that *Summers* also relied on the limited intrusion on personal liberty involved with detaining occupants incident to the execution of a search warrant. It concluded that where officers arrest an individual away from his or her home, there is an additional level of intrusiveness. The Court declined to precisely define the term "immediate vicinity," leaving it to the lower courts to make this determination based on "the lawful limits of the premises, whether the occupant was within the line of sight of his dwelling, the ease of reentry from the occupant's location, and other relevant factors."

Frisking People Present (page 472)

State v. Richmond, 215 N.C. App. 475, 481, 482 (2011). An officer was present at a location to execute a search warrant in connection with drug offenses. The court of appeals ruled that evidence supported the trial court's finding that the officer, based on his training and experience, immediately formed the opinion during a pat-down that a bulge in the defendant's pants contained a controlled substance. Although the officer testified that he felt a "knot" in the defendant's pants that he could not "describe with any specificity," the officer also testified that he had discovered similar knots before in his six years of experience and had previously discovered "[b]ags of marijuana, bags of cocaine, bags of crack."

Challenging the Validity of a Search Warrant (page 479)

Revelation of a Confidential Informant's Identity at a Suppression Hearing or Trial (page 481)

NORTH CAROLINA COURT OF APPEALS (page 481)

State v. Avent, ___ N.C. App. ___, 729 S.E.2d 708 (2012). The trial court did not err by denying the defendant's motion to compel disclosure of the identity of a confidential informant who provided the defendant's cell phone number to the police. Applying *Roviaro v. United States,* 353 U.S. 53 (1957), the court noted that the defendant failed to show or allege that the informant participated in the crime, and the evidence did not contradict material facts that the informant could clarify. Although the State asserted that the defendant was the shooter in the murder being tried and the defendant asserted that he was not at the scene, the defendant failed to show how the informant's identity would be relevant to this issue. Additionally, evidence independent of the informant's testimony established the defendant's guilt, including an eyewitness to the murder.

State v. Mack, 214 N.C. App. 169 (2011). The trial court did not err by denying the defendant's motion to disclose the identity of a confidential informant in a drug case when the defendant failed to show that the circumstances of his case required disclosure. The informant was not a participant in the crime—he introduced the defendant to the undercover police officer and then stood aside while they haggled about the price of the drugs. The defendant did not need the informant's testimony at trial, despite his argument (1) that the informant could have testified that he (the defendant) was not the person who sold the drugs to the officer because other people were present in the house when the drug sale occurred and (2) that the informant also could have testified about the officer's allegedly mistaken identification of the defendant. The officer had clearly identified the defendant as the person who sold him the drugs.

State v. Ellison, 213 N.C. App. 300 (2011), *aff'd on other grounds*, 366 N.C. 439 (2013). The trial court did not err by denying the defendant's motion for disclosure of an informant's identity when the informant's existence was sufficiently corroborated under G.S. 15A-978(b). A second officer testified that the principal investigating officer had told her about information that he had gained from a "tipster" concerning an illegal drug transaction, and she confirmed the truth of the information through her own investigation.

Possible Defects in a Search Warrant or the Procedure in Issuing a Search Warrant (page 483)

State v. Rayfield, ___ N.C. App. ___, 752 S.E.2d 745 (2014). The court ruled in a child sex case that although the magistrate violated G.S. 15A-245 by considering an officer's sworn testimony when determining whether probable cause supported a search warrant but failing to record that testimony as required by the statute, this violation was not a sufficient basis to grant the defendant's suppression motion. The trial court had based its ruling solely on the filed affidavit, not the sworn testimony, and the affidavit was sufficient to establish probable cause.

IV. Suppression Motions and Hearings; Exclusionary Rules (page 500)

Trial Court's Ruling on Suppression Motion (page 502)

Trial Court's Findings of Fact and Conclusions of Law (page 503)

State v. Bartlett, ___ N.C. App. ___, 752 S.E.2d 237 (2013). The court ruled that a written order is not required for a suppression motion when the trial court gives its rationale from the bench and there are no material conflicts in the evidence. Thus, the court determined that it need not reach the issue of whether a judge who had not heard the evidence at the suppression hearing had authority to sign a written order granting the suppression motion.

State v. Morgan, ___ N.C. App. ___, 741 S.E.2d 422 (2013). The trial court erred by failing to issue a written order denying the defendant's motion to suppress. A written order is necessary unless the court announces its rationale from the bench and there are no material conflicts in the evidence. Although the trial court announced its ruling from the bench, there was a material conflict in the evidence. The court remanded for the entry of a written order.

State v. O'Connor, ___ N.C. App. ___, ___, 730 S.E.2d 248, 253 (2012). In granting the defendant's motion to suppress, the trial court erred by failing to make findings of fact resolving material conflicts in the evidence. The court of appeals rejected the defendant's argument that the trial court "indirectly provided a rationale from the bench" by stating that the motion was granted for the reasons in the defendant's memorandum.

State v. Salinas, 366 N.C. 119 (2012). Modifying and affirming *State v. Salinas*, 214 N.C. App. 408 (2011) (trial court incorrectly applied a probable cause standard instead of a reasonable suspicion standard to a vehicle stop), the state supreme court ruled that the trial court may not rely on allegations contained in a defendant's G.S. 15A-977(a) affidavit when making findings of fact in connection with a motion to suppress.

Law of the Case (new topic to be inserted on page 503)

State v. Lewis, 365 N.C. 488, 505 (2012). Affirming the court of appeals, the state supreme court ruled that on a retrial the trial court erred by applying the law of the case and denying the defendant's motion to suppress. At the defendant's first trial, he unsuccessfully moved to suppress the victim's identification as unduly suggestive. That issue was affirmed on appeal. At the retrial, the defense filed new motions to suppress on the same grounds. However, at the pretrial hearings on these motions, the defense introduced new evidence relevant to the reliability of the identification. The State successfully argued that the law of the case governed and that the defendant's motions must be denied. After the defendant was again convicted, he appealed, and the court of appeals reversed on this issue. Affirming that ruling, the supreme court noted that "the law of the case doctrine does not apply when the evidence presented at a subsequent proceeding is different from that presented on a former appeal." It then affirmed the court of appeals' ruling that the trial court erred in applying the doctrine of the law of the case to the defendant's motion to suppress at the retrial.

Suppression Hearings (page 504)

State v. Williams, ___ N.C. App. ___, 738 S.E.2d 211 (2013). The court of appeals ruled that the trial court did not impermissibly place the burden of proof on the defendant at a suppression hearing. Initially, the burden is on the defendant to show that a suppression motion is timely and in proper form. The burden then is on the State to demonstrate the admissibility of the challenged evidence. The party who bears the burden of proof typically presents evidence first. In this case, the fact that the defendant presented evidence first at the suppression hearing does not by itself establish that the burden of proof was shifted to the defendant.

Appellate Review of Suppression Motions and Rulings (page 505)

State v. Oates, 366 N.C. 264, 266 (2012). The state supreme court reversed the decision below, 215 N.C. App. 491 (2011), and ruled that the State's notice of appeal of a trial court ruling on a suppression motion was timely. The State's notice was filed seven days after the trial judge in open court orally granted the defendant's pretrial motion to suppress, but three months before the trial judge issued his corresponding written order of suppression. The supreme court ruled that the window for filing a written notice of appeal in a criminal case opens on the date of rendition of the judgment or order and closes fourteen days after entry of the judgment or order. The court clarified that rendering a judgment or an order means to pronounce, state, declare, or announce the judgment or order and is "the judicial act of the court in pronouncing the sentence of the law upon the facts in controversy." Entering a judgment or an order is "a ministerial act which consists in spreading it upon the record." It continued:

> For the purposes of entering notice of appeal in a criminal case . . . a judgment or an order is rendered when the judge decides the issue before him or her and advises the necessary individuals of the decision; a judgment or an order is entered under that Rule when the clerk of court records or files the judge's decision regarding the judgment or order.

State v. Brown, 217 N.C. App. 566, 568 (2011). The court of appeals ruled that the defendant gave sufficient notice of his intent to appeal the denial of his motion to suppress to preserve his right to appeal. The State had argued that defense counsel's language was not specific enough to place the trial court and prosecution on notice of his intention to appeal the adverse ruling. Immediately following an attempt to make a renewed motion to suppress at the end of the State's evidence, defense counsel stated "that [the defendant] would like to preserve any appellate issues that may stem from the motions in this trial." The court of appeals noted that the defendant had only made five motions during trial, two of which were motions to suppress, and that following defense counsel's request, the trial court reentered substantially similar facts to the ones it entered when initially denying the pretrial motion to suppress. Clearly, the court concluded, the trial court understood which motion the defendant intended to appeal and decided to make its findings of fact as clear as possible for the record.

General Exclusionary Rules (page 514)

The Inevitable-Discovery Exception (page 520)

NORTH CAROLINA COURT OF APPEALS (page 521)

State v. Wells, ___ N.C. App. ___, 737 S.E.2d 179 (2013). In a case in which the defendant was convicted of soliciting a child by computer and attempted indecent liberties on a child, the court of appeals ruled that the trial court erred by concluding that the defendant's laptop would have been inevitably discovered. The trial court ordered suppressed statements the defendant made to officers during questioning. In those statements, the defendant told officers that he owned a laptop that was located on his bed at the fire station. The trial court denied the defendant's motion to suppress evidence retrieved from his laptop, concluding that it would have been inevitably discovered. The court of appeals found that the State had not presented any evidence—from the investigating officers or anyone else—supporting this conclusion.

Exclusionary Rule for Chapter 20 Violations (new section to be inserted after "North Carolina's Statutory Exclusionary Rule" on page 525)

State v. White, ___ N.C. App. ___, 753 S.E.2d 698 (2014). The court ruled that the trial court did not err by granting the defendant's motion to suppress evidence obtained as a result of a vehicle checkpoint. Specifically, the trial court did not err by concluding that a lack of a written policy in full force and effect at the time of the defendant's stop at the checkpoint constituted a substantial violation of G.S. 20-16.3A(a)(2a) (requiring a written policy providing guidelines for checkpoints). The court also rejected the State's argument that a substantial violation of G.S. 20-16.3A could not support suppression; the State had argued that evidence only can be suppressed if there is a constitutional violation or a substantial violation of G.S. Chapter 15A. The court noted that G.S. 20-16.3A(d) specifically bars the suppression of evidence for a violation of subsection (d) (placement of checkpoints) but that suppression is not prohibited for a violation of subdivision (a)(2a), which requires a written checkpoint policy. The court reasoned that these differences reflect a legislative intent to authorize suppression for a violation of subdivision (a)(2a). In any event, the court noted that other cases have upheld suppression of evidence for a Chapter 20 violation despite the lack of express statutory authorization to suppress evidence. *See* State v. Buckheit, ___ N.C. App. ___, 735 S.E.2d 345 (2012) (suppressing evidence for violation of G.S. 20-16.2(a)); State v. Hatley, 190 N.C. App. 639 (2008) (similar ruling).

Chapter 5

Interrogation and Confessions, Lineups and Other Identification Procedures, and Undercover Officers and Informants

Chapter 5

Interrogation and Confessions, Lineups and Other Identification Procedures, and Undercover Officers and Informants

Part I. Interrogation and Confessions (page 529)

Voluntariness of the Defendant's Statement (page 533)

Footnote 31 (page 533)

Add the following case to footnote 31: Bobby v. Dixon, 132 S. Ct. 26 (2011) (officers' urging defendant to "cut a deal" before his accomplice did so did not cause resulting confession to be involuntary).

Footnote 33 (page 534)

Add the following case to footnote 33: State v. Martin, ___ N.C. App. ___, 746 S.E.2d 307 (2013) (officer improperly suggested that he was in a position to offer plea arrangement on defendant's behalf).

The *Miranda* Rule and Additional Statutory Rights (page 534)

Overview (page 534)

Deliberate Technique of Question Arrestee First, Give Miranda Warnings Later (page 537)

Footnote 53 (page 537)

Add the following case discussion to footnote 53: In *Bobby v. Dixon*, 132 S. Ct. 26 (2011), the Court determined that there was no *Seibert* violation. The nature of the interrogation in the case was different than in *Seibert*. Here, the Court explained, the defendant denied involvement in the murder and then, after *Miranda* warnings were given, changed his mind and confessed; in *Seibert* the defendant confessed both times. Additionally, the Court noted, in contrast to *Seibert*, the two interrogations at issue here did not occur in one continuum. To read more about the case, see the summary of *Bobby v. Dixon* in the Chapter 5 case summaries appendix in this supplement.

When the *Miranda* Rule Applies: Custody and Interrogation (page 537)

The Meaning of "Custody" (page 537)

Inmate in jail or prison (page 539)

In *Howes v. Fields,*[1] the United States Supreme Court ruled that a federal appellate court erroneously concluded that a prisoner was in custody under *Miranda* when the prisoner was taken aside and questioned about events that occurred

---

1. 132 S. Ct. 1181 (2012).

outside the prison. The prisoner (Fields) was escorted by a correction officer to a conference room where two sheriff's deputies questioned him about allegations that, before he came to prison, he had engaged in sexual conduct with a 12-year-old boy. To get to the conference room, Fields had to go down one floor and pass through a locked door that separated two sections of the facility. Fields arrived at the conference room between 7:00 and 9:00 p.m. and was questioned for about five to seven hours. At the beginning of the interview, Fields was told that he was free to leave and return to his cell. Later, he was again told that he could leave whenever he wanted. The interviewing deputies were armed, but Fields remained free of handcuffs and other restraints. The door to the conference room was sometimes open and sometimes shut. About halfway through the interview, after Fields had been confronted with the allegations of abuse, he became agitated and began to yell. One of the deputies, using an expletive, told Fields to sit down and said that "if [he] didn't want to cooperate, [he] could leave."[2] Fields eventually confessed to engaging in sex acts with the boy. Fields asserted that he said several times during the interview that he no longer wanted to talk to the deputies, but he did not ask to go back to his cell before the interview ended. When he was eventually ready to leave, he had to wait an additional twenty minutes or so because an officer had to be called to escort him back to his cell, and he did not return to his cell until well after the time he generally went to bed. Fields was never given *Miranda* warnings or advised that he did not have to speak with the deputies. Fields was charged with criminal sexual conduct. He unsuccessfully moved to suppress his confession, and the jury convicted him of criminal sexual conduct. After an unsuccessful direct appeal, Fields filed for federal habeas relief. The federal district court granted relief and the Sixth Circuit affirmed, ruling that the interview was a custodial interrogation because isolation from the general prison population, combined with questioning about conduct occurring outside the prison, made any interrogation automatically custodial. Reversing, the Supreme Court stated the following: "[I]t is abundantly clear that our precedents do not clearly establish the categorical rule on which the Court of Appeals relied, i.e., that the questioning of a prisoner is always custodial when the prisoner is removed from the general prison population and questioned about events that occurred outside the prison." "On the contrary," the Court added, "we have repeatedly declined to adopt any categorical rule with respect to whether the questioning of a prison inmate is custodial."[3] The Court ruled that based on the facts presented, Fields was not in custody under *Miranda*.

Age of a juvenile (page 540)

Footnote 69 (page 540)

Add the following case summaries to footnote 69: *See also In re* A.N.C., Jr., ___ N.C. App. ___, 750 S.E.2d 835 (2013) (court ruled that a 13-year-old juvenile was not in custody within the meaning of G.S. 7B-2101 or *Miranda* during a roadside questioning by an officer; noting that under *J.D.B. v. North Carolina*, 131 S. Ct. 2394 (2011), a reviewing court must, when determining whether a suspect has been placed in custody, take into account a juvenile's age if it was known to an officer or would have been objectively apparent to a reasonable officer, the court nevertheless concluded that the juvenile was not in custody); State v. Yancey, ___ N.C. App. ___, 727 S.E.2d 382 (2012) (court ruled that the juvenile defendant was not in custody for purposes of *Miranda* when questioned in an unmarked law enforcement vehicle by two detectives dressed in plain clothes; the juvenile was 17 years and 10 months old; considering the totality of the circumstances—including the defendant's age—the court concluded that the defendant was not in custody; the court rejected the argument that *J.D.B.*, cited *supra* in this paragraph, required a different conclusion).

A Defendant's Assertion of the Right to Remain Silent and the Right to Counsel (page 542)

Asserting the Right to Remain Silent (page 543)

Similar to the discussion on page 543 under "Asserting the Right to Counsel," a defendant's assertion of the right to remain silent before he or she is in custody, like the assertion of the right to counsel under similar circumstances, is likely not a proper assertion.[4]

---

2. *Id.* at 1186.

3. *Id.* at 1187.

4. In *Bobby v. Dixon*, 132 S. Ct. 26 (2011), the United States Supreme Court stated that it had never ruled that a person can invoke *Miranda* rights anticipatorily in a context other than custodial interrogation.

Asserting the Right to Counsel (page 543)

When assertion of right to counsel may be made (page 543)

Footnote 90 (page 543)

Add the following discussion to footnote 90: In *Bobby v. Dixon,* 132 S. Ct. 26 (2011), the United States Supreme Court stated that it had never ruled that a person can invoke *Miranda* rights anticipatorily in a context other than custodial interrogation.

Resumption of Interrogation after the Defendant's Assertion of Rights (page 545)

The Right to Counsel (page 546)

Maryland v. Shatzer and break in custody permitting reinterrogation (page 547)

Footnote 116 (page 549)

Add to footnote 116: The court in *United States v. Ellison,* 632 F.3d 727, 730 (1st Cir. 2010), noted that *Shatzer* left open the question of whether its ruling applied to a defendant in pretrial custody for other charges.

Part II. Lineups and Other Identification Procedures (page 557)

Nonsuggestiveness of the Identification Procedure under Due Process Clause (page 558)

In *Perry v. New Hampshire,*[5] the United States Supreme Court ruled that the Due Process Clause does not require a preliminary judicial inquiry into the reliability of an eyewitness identification when the identification was not procured under unnecessarily suggestive circumstances arranged by law enforcement. The Court stated: "When no improper law enforcement activity is involved . . . it suffices to test reliability through the rights and opportunities generally designed for that purpose, notably, the presence of counsel at postindictment lineups, vigorous cross-examination, protective rules of evidence, and jury instructions on both the fallibility of eyewitness identification and the requirement that guilt be proved beyond a reasonable doubt."[6]

North Carolina Statutory Procedures for Live Lineups and Photo Lineups (page 561)

In *State v. Stowes,*[7] the North Carolina Court of Appeals ruled that the trial court did not commit plain error by granting the defendant relief under the Eyewitness Identification Reform Act (EIRA), while not excluding evidence of a pretrial identification. The trial court found that an EIRA violation occurred because one of the officers administering the identification procedure was involved in the investigation. The court concluded: "We are not persuaded that the trial court committed plain error by granting Defendant all other available remedies under EIRA, rather than excluding the evidence."[8]

---

5. 132 S. Ct. 716 (2012).
6. *Id.* at 721.
7. ___ N.C. App. ___, 727 S.E.2d 351 (2012).
8. ___ N. C. App. at ___, 727 S.E.2d at 358.

Chapter 5 Appendix: Case Summaries

Chapter 5 Appendix: Case Summaries

I. Interrogation and Confessions (page 573)

Voluntariness of the Defendant's Statement (page 573)

NORTH CAROLINA COURT OF APPEALS (page 575)

State v. Martin, ___ N.C. App. ___, 746 S.E.2d 307 (2013). The court ruled that the defendant's confession was involuntary. The defendant first made a confession before *Miranda* warnings were given. The officer then gave the defendant *Miranda* warnings and had the defendant repeat his confession. The trial court suppressed the defendant's pre-*Miranda* confession but ruled that the post-*Miranda* confession was admissible. The appeals court disagreed, concluding that the circumstances and tactics used by the officer to induce the first confession must be imputed to the post-*Miranda* confession. The court found the first confession involuntary, noting that the defendant was in custody; the officer made misrepresentations and/or deceptive statements, as well as promises to induce the confession; and the defendant may have had an impaired mental condition.

State v. Rollins, ___ N.C. App. ___, 738 S.E.2d 440 (2013). The court of appeals ruled that the trial court did not err by finding that the defendant's statements to his wife regarding his participation in a murder were voluntary. The defendant's wife spoke with him five times while he was in prison (on charges not connected to the murder) and while wearing a recording device provided by the police. While the wife did not threaten the defendant, she did make up evidence which she claimed law enforcement had recovered and told the defendant that officers suspected that she was involved in the murder. In response, the defendant made incriminating statements in which he corrected the wife's lies concerning the evidence and admitted details of the murder. The court rejected the defendant's argument that his statements were involuntary because of his wife's deception and her emotional appeals to him based on this deception.

State v. Graham, ___ N.C. App. ___, 733 S.E.2d 100 (2012). The court ruled in this child sexual abuse trial that the defendant's confession was not involuntary. After briefly speaking to the defendant at his home about an allegation of child sexual abuse against him, an officer asked him to come to the police station to answer questions. The court rejected the defendant's argument that his subsequent confession was involuntary because he was given a false hope of leniency if he were to confess and because he was told that additional charges would stem from continued investigation of other children. The officers' offers to "help" the defendant "deal with" his "problem" did not constitute a direct promise that the defendant would receive a lesser—or even no—charge should he confess. The court also rejected the defendant's argument that the confession was involuntary because one of the officers relied on his friendship with the defendant and their shared racial background and because another officer asked questions about whether the defendant went to church or believed in God. Finally, the court rejected the defendant's argument that his confession was involuntarily obtained through deception.

State v. Cornelius, ___ N.C. App. ___, 723 S.E.2d 783 (2012). The court of appeals ruled that the trial court did not err by denying the defendant's motion to suppress three statements made while he was in the hospital. The defendant had argued that medication he received rendered the statements involuntary. Based on testimony of the detective who conducted the interview, hospital records, and the recorded statements, the trial court made extensive findings that the defendant was alert and oriented. Those findings supported the trial court's conclusion that the statements were voluntary.

State v. Cooper, ___ N.C. App. ___, 723 S.E.2d 780 (2012). The court of appeals rejected the defendant's argument that his confession was involuntary because it was obtained through police threats. Although the defendant argued that the police threatened to imprison his father unless he confessed, the trial court's findings of fact were more than sufficient to support its conclusion that the confession was not coerced. The trial court found, in part, that the defendant never was promised or told that his father would benefit from any statements that he himself made.

Use of Deception (page 577)

State v. Rollins, ___ N.C. App. ___, 738 S.E.2d 440 (2013). The court of appeals ruled that the trial court did not err by finding that the defendant's statements to his wife regarding his participation in a murder were voluntary. The defendant's wife spoke with him five times while he was in prison (on charges not connected to the murder) and while wearing a recording device provided by the police. While the wife did not threaten the defendant, she did make up evidence which she claimed law enforcement had recovered and told the defendant that officers suspected that she was involved in the murder. In response, the defendant made incriminating statements in which he corrected the wife's lies concerning the evidence and admitted details of the murder. The court rejected the defendant's argument that his statements were involuntary because of his wife's deception and her emotional appeals to him based on this deception.

Confession Made after an Involuntary Confession (page 578)

State v. Martin, ___ N.C. App. ___, 746 S.E.2d 307 (2013). The court ruled that the defendant's confession was involuntary. The defendant first made a confession before *Miranda* warnings were given. The officer then gave the defendant *Miranda* warnings and had the defendant repeat his confession. The trial court suppressed the defendant's pre-*Miranda* confession but ruled that the post-*Miranda* confession was admissible. The appeals court disagreed, concluding that the circumstances and tactics used by the officer to induce the first confession must be imputed to the post-*Miranda* confession. The court found the first confession involuntary, noting that the defendant was in custody; the officer made misrepresentations or deceptive statements, as well as promises to induce the confession; and the defendant may have had an impaired mental condition.

Defendant's Statements: *Miranda* Warnings and Waiver (page 578)

NORTH CAROLINA COURT OF APPEALS (page 580)

State v. Quick, ___ N.C. App. ___, 739 S.E.2d 608 (2013). The court of appeals rejected the State's argument that the defendant initiated contact with the police following his initial request for counsel and thus waived his right to counsel. After the defendant asserted his right to counsel, the police returned him to the interrogation room and again asked if he wanted counsel; he said yes. Then, on the way from the interrogation room back to the jail, a detective told the defendant that an attorney would not be able to help him and that he would be served with warrants regardless of whether an attorney was there. The police knew or should have known that telling the defendant that an attorney could not help him with the warrants would be reasonably likely to elicit an incriminating response. It was only after this statement by police that the defendant agreed to talk. Therefore, the court of appeals concluded, the defendant did not initiate the communication. The court also concluded that even if the defendant had initiated communication with police, his waiver was not knowing and intelligent. The trial court had found that the prosecution failed to meet its burden of showing that the defendant made a knowing and intelligent waiver, relying on the facts that the defendant was 18 years old and had limited experience with the criminal justice system. There was a period of time between 12:39 and 12:54 p.m. on the day the defendant was questioned when there was no evidence as to what occurred and no audio or video recording of the interview. The court found that the defendant's age and inexperience, when combined with the circumstances of his interrogation, supported the trial court's conclusion that the State failed to prove the defendant's waiver was knowing and intelligent.

State v. Cureton, ___ N.C. App. ___, 734 S.E.2d 572 (2012). The court ruled that the defendant knowingly and intelligently waived his right to counsel after being read his *Miranda* rights. The court rejected the defendant's argument that the fact that he never signed the waiver of rights form had established that a valid waiver was not made. The court also rejected the defendant's argument that he was incapable of knowingly and intelligently waiving his rights because his borderline mental capacity prevented him from fully understanding those rights. The court relied in part on a psychological evaluation diagnosing the defendant as malingering and finding him competent to stand trial.

Questioning by Non–Law Enforcement Officers (page 590)

State v. Rollins, ___ N.C. App. ___, 738 S.E.2d 440 (2013). The court ruled that the trial court did not err by finding that the defendant's statements to his wife regarding his participation in a murder were voluntary. The defendant's wife spoke with him five times while he was in prison (on charges not connected to the murder) and while wearing a recording device provided by the police. While the wife did not threaten the defendant, she did make up evidence which she claimed law enforcement had recovered and told the defendant that officers suspected that she was involved in the murder. In response, the defendant made incriminating statements in which he corrected the wife's lies concerning the evidence and admitted details of the murder. The court rejected the defendant's argument that his statements were involuntary because of his wife's deception and her emotional appeals to him based on this deception.

The Meaning of "Custody" under *Miranda* (page 592)

Generally (page 592)

NORTH CAROLINA COURT OF APPEALS (page 599)

State v. Price, ___ N.C. App. ___, 757 S.E.2d 309 (2014). The court ruled that the trial court erred by granting the defendant's motion to suppress. A wildlife officer on patrol in a pine forest approached the defendant, who was dressed in full camouflage and carrying a hunting rifle, and asked to see his hunting license. After the defendant showed his license, the officer asked how he got to the location; he replied that his wife transported him there. The officer then asked him whether he was a convicted felon. The defendant admitted that he was. The officer seized the weapon, and the defendant was later charged with being a felon in possession of a firearm. The court ruled that the defendant was neither seized under the Fourth Amendment nor in custody under *Miranda* when the officer asked about his criminal history, and therefore the trial court erred by granting the motion to suppress.

In re A.N.C., Jr., ___ N.C. App. ___, 750 S.E.2d 835 (2013). The court ruled that a 13-year-old juvenile was not in custody within the meaning of G.S. 7B-2101 or *Miranda* during a roadside questioning by an officer. Responding to a report of a vehicle accident, the officer saw the wrecked vehicle, which had crashed into a utility pole, and three people walking from the scene. When the officer questioned all three, the juvenile admitted that he had been driving the wrecked vehicle. Noting that under *J.D.B. v. North Carolina,* 131 S. Ct. 2394 (2011), a reviewing court must, when determining whether a suspect has been placed in custody, take into account a juvenile's age if it was known to an officer or would have been objectively apparent to a reasonable officer, the court nevertheless concluded that the juvenile here was not in custody.

State v. Yancey, ___ N.C. App. ___, 727 S.E.2d 382 (2012). The court ruled that the juvenile defendant was not in custody for purposes of *Miranda.* After the defendant had been identified as a possible suspect in several breaking or entering cases, two detectives dressed in plain clothes and driving an unmarked vehicle went to the defendant's home and asked to speak with him. Because the defendant had friends visiting his home, the detectives asked the defendant to take a ride in their car with them. The detectives told the defendant that he was free to leave at any time, and they did not touch him. The defendant sat in the front seat of the vehicle while it was driven approximately two miles from his home. When the vehicle stopped, one of the detectives showed the defendant reports of the break-ins. The detectives told the defendant that if he was cooperative, they would not arrest him that day. The defendant admitted to committing the break-ins. The juvenile was 17 years and 10 months old. Considering the totality of the circumstances—including the defendant's age—the court concluded that the defendant was not in custody. The court rejected the argument that *J.D.B. v. North Carolina,* 131 S. Ct. 2394 (2011), required a different conclusion.

State v. Hemphill, ___ N.C. App. ___, 723 S.E.2d 142 (2012). The court ruled that the defendant's response to an officer's questioning while on the ground and being restrained with handcuffs should have been suppressed because the defendant had not been given *Miranda* warnings. The officer's questioning constituted an interrogation, and a reasonable person in the defendant's position—having been forced to the ground by an officer with a TASER® drawn and in the process of being handcuffed—would have felt that his or her freedom of movement had been restrained to a degree associated with formal arrest. Thus, there was a custodial interrogation.

Prisoners and Jail Inmates (page 606)

Howes v. Fields, 132 S. Ct. 1181, 1186, 1187 (2012). The United States Supreme Court ruled that a federal appellate court erroneously concluded that a prisoner was in custody under *Miranda* when the prisoner was taken aside and questioned about events that occurred outside the prison. The prisoner (Fields) was escorted by a correction officer to a conference room where two sheriff's deputies questioned him about allegations that, before he came to prison, he had engaged in sexual conduct with a 12-year-old boy. To get to the conference room, Fields had to go down one floor and pass through a locked door that separated two sections of the facility. Fields arrived at the conference room between 7:00 and 9:00 p.m. and was questioned for about five to seven hours. At the beginning of the interview, Fields was told that he was free to leave and return to his cell. Later, he was again told that he could leave whenever he wanted. The interviewing deputies were armed, but Fields remained free of handcuffs and other restraints. The door to the conference room was sometimes open and sometimes shut. About halfway through the interview, after Fields had been confronted with the allegations of abuse, he became agitated and began to yell. One of the deputies, using an expletive, told Fields to sit down and said that "if [he] didn't want to cooperate, [he] could leave." Fields eventually confessed to engaging in sex acts with the boy. Fields asserted that he said several times during the interview that he no longer wanted to talk to the deputies but that he did not ask to go back to his cell before the interview ended. When he was eventually ready to leave, he had to wait an additional twenty minutes or so because an officer had to be called to escort him back to his cell, and he did not return to his cell until well after the time he generally went to bed. Fields was never given *Miranda* warnings or advised that he did not have to speak with the deputies. Fields was charged with criminal sexual conduct. He unsuccessfully moved to suppress his confession, and the jury convicted him of criminal sexual conduct. After an unsuccessful direct appeal, Fields filed for federal habeas relief. The federal district court granted relief and the Sixth Circuit affirmed, ruling that the interview was a custodial interrogation because isolation from the general prison population, combined with questioning about conduct occurring outside the prison, made any interrogation automatically custodial. Reversing, the Supreme Court stated: "[I]t is abundantly clear that our precedents do not clearly establish the categorical rule on which the Court of Appeals relied, *i.e.,* that the questioning of a prisoner is always custodial when the prisoner is removed from the general prison population and questioned about events that occurred outside the prison." "On the contrary," the Court stated, "we have repeatedly declined to adopt any categorical rule with respect to whether the questioning of a prison inmate is custodial." The Court ruled that based on the facts presented, Fields was not in custody under *Miranda.*

Juveniles (page 606)

In re A.N.C., Jr., ___ N.C. App. ___, 750 S.E.2d 835 (2013). The court ruled that a 13-year-old juvenile was not in custody within the meaning of G.S. 7B-2101 or *Miranda* during a roadside questioning by an officer. Responding to a report of a vehicle accident, the officer saw the wrecked vehicle, which had crashed into a utility pole, and three people walking from the scene. When the officer questioned all three, the juvenile admitted that he had been driving the wrecked vehicle. Noting that under *J.D.B. v. North Carolina,* 131 S. Ct. 2394 (2011), a reviewing court must, when determining whether a suspect has been placed in custody, take into account a juvenile's age if it was known to an officer or would have been objectively apparent to a reasonable officer, the court nevertheless concluded that the juvenile here was not in custody.

State v. Yancey, ___ N.C. App. ___, 727 S.E.2d 382 (2012). The juvenile defendant was not in custody for purposes of *Miranda.* After the defendant had been identified as a possible suspect in several breaking or entering cases, two detectives dressed in plain clothes and driving an unmarked vehicle went to the defendant's home and asked to speak with him. Because the defendant had friends visiting his home, the detectives asked the defendant to take a ride in their car with them. The detectives told the defendant that he was free to leave at any time, and they did not touch him. The defendant sat in the front seat of the vehicle while it was driven approximately two miles from his home. When the vehicle stopped, one of the detectives showed the defendant reports of the break-ins. The detectives told the defendant that if he was cooperative, they would not arrest him that day. The defendant admitted to committing the break-ins. The juvenile was 17 years and 10 months old. Considering the totality of the circumstances—including the defendant's age—the court concluded that the defendant was not in custody. The court rejected the argument that *J.D.B. v. North Carolina*, 131 S. Ct. 2394 (2011), required a different conclusion.

The Meaning of "Interrogation" under *Miranda* (page 609)
Generally (page 609)
NORTH CAROLINA COURT OF APPEALS (page 611)

State v. Hogan, ___ N.C. App. ___, ___, 758 S.E.2d 465, 471 (2014). The court ruled that the defendant's statements, made while a law enforcement officer who had responded to a domestic violence call questioned the defendant's girlfriend in his presence (the officer asked how she got marks that were visible on her neck), were spontaneous and not in response to interrogation. The State conceded that the defendant was in custody at the time. The court rejected the defendant's argument that asking his girlfriend what happened in front of him was a coercive technique designed to elicit an incriminating statement. Acknowledging that the "case is a close one," the court concluded that the officer's question to the girlfriend did not constitute the functional equivalent of questioning the defendant; the officer's question did not call for a response from the defendant, and therefore it was not reasonably likely to elicit an incriminating response from him.

Assertion of *Miranda* Rights (page 616)
Assertion of the Right to Counsel (page 620)
NORTH CAROLINA COURT OF APPEALS (page 630)

State v. Quick, ___ N.C. App. ___, 739 S.E.2d 608 (2013). The court rejected the State's argument that the defendant initiated contact with the police following his initial request for counsel and thus waived his right to counsel. After the defendant asserted his right to counsel, the police returned him to the interrogation room and again asked if he wanted counsel; he said yes. Then, on the way from the interrogation room back to the jail, a detective told the defendant that an attorney would not be able to help him and that he would be served with warrants regardless of whether an attorney was there. The police knew or should have known that telling the defendant that an attorney could not help him with the warrants would be reasonably likely to elicit an incriminating response. It was only after this statement by police that the defendant agreed to talk. Therefore, the court concluded, the defendant did not initiate the communication. The court also concluded that even if the defendant had initiated communication with police, his waiver was not knowing and intelligent. The trial court had found that the prosecution failed to meet its burden of showing that the defendant made a knowing and intelligent waiver, relying on the facts that the defendant was 18 years old and had limited experience with the criminal justice system. There was a period of time between 12:39 and 12:54 p.m. on the day the defendant was questioned when there was no evidence as to what occurred and no audio or video recording of the interview. The court found that the defendant's age and inexperience, when combined with the circumstances of his interrogation, supported the trial court's conclusion that the State failed to prove the defendant's waiver was knowing and intelligent.

State v. Cureton, ___ N.C. App. ___, ___, 734 S.E.2d 572, 582 (2012). The court ruled that the defendant did not unambiguously ask to speak to a lawyer. The court rejected the defendant's argument that he made a clear request for counsel, concluding as follows: "Defendant never expressed a clear desire to speak with an attorney. Rather, he appears to have been seeking clarification regarding whether he had a right to speak with an attorney before answering any of the detective's questions." The court added: "There is a distinct difference between inquiring whether one has the right to counsel and actually requesting counsel. Once defendant was informed that it was his decision whether to invoke the right to counsel, he opted not to exercise that right."

Evidentiary Use of a Defendant's Silence or Assertion of Right to Counsel or Right to Remain Silent (page 634)

UNITED STATES SUPREME COURT (page 634)

Salinas v. Texas, 133 S. Ct. 2174, 2178 (2013). The Court ruled that the use at trial of the defendant's silence during a non-custodial interview did not violate the Fifth Amendment. Without being placed in custody or receiving *Miranda* warnings, the defendant voluntarily answered an officer's questions about a murder. But when asked whether his shotgun would match shells recovered at the murder scene, the defendant declined to answer. Instead, he looked at the floor, shuffled his feet, bit his bottom lip, clenched his hands in his lap, and began "to tighten up." After a few moments, the officer asked additional questions, which the defendant answered. The defendant was charged with murder, and at trial prosecutors argued that his reaction to the officer's question suggested that he was guilty. A three-Justice plurality found it unnecessary to reach the primary issue, concluding instead that the defendant's argument that the prosecutor's jury argument based on the defendant's silence violated his Fifth Amendment privilege against self-incrimination failed because he did not expressly invoke the privilege in response to the officer's question, and no exception applied to excuse his failure to invoke the privilege. A separate two-Justice plurality concurred in the judgment but for a different reason: the defendant's argument would fail even if he had invoked the privilege because the prosecutor's comments regarding his pre-custodial silence did not compel him to give self-incriminating testimony. [*Author's note*: Because the three-Justice plurality represents the narrower ground to reverse the judgment, it is the controlling opinion. *See* Marks v. United States, 430 U.S. 188, 193 (1977) (when a fragmented Court decides a case and no single rationale explaining the result enjoys the assent of five Justices, the holding of the Court may be viewed as the position taken by the Justices who concurred in the judgment on the narrowest grounds.)]

NORTH CAROLINA SUPREME COURT (page 635)

State v. Moore, 366 N.C. 100, 105 (2012). On direct examination an officer testified that after he read the defendant his *Miranda* rights, the defendant "refused to talk about the case." Because this testimony referred to the defendant's exercise of his right to silence, its admission was error. The court rejected the State's argument that no error occurred because the comments were neither made by the prosecutor nor the result of a question by the prosecutor designed to elicit a comment on the defendant's exercise of his right to silence. The court stated: "An improper adverse inference of guilt from a defendant's exercise of his right to remain silent cannot be made, regardless of who comments on it."

NORTH CAROLINA COURT OF APPEALS (page 636)

State v. Barbour, ___ N.C. App. ___, 748 S.E.2d 59 (2013). The court ruled that the State did not impermissibly present evidence of the defendant's post-*Miranda* silence. After being advised of his *Miranda* rights, the defendant did not remain silent but, rather, made statements to the police. Thus, no error occurred when an officer indicated that after his arrest the defendant never asked to speak with the officer or anyone else in the officer's agency.

State v. Harrison, ___ N.C. App. ___, ___, 721 S.E.2d 371, 379 (2012). The court of appeals ruled that the trial court committed error by allowing the State to use the defendant's pre- and post-arrest silence as substantive evidence of guilt. When explaining the circumstances of the defendant's initial interview, an officer testifying for the State stated: "He provided me—he denied any involvement, wished to give me no statement, written or verbal." Also, when the State asked the officer whether the defendant had made any statements after arrest, the officer responded, "After he was mirandized [*sic*], he waived his rights and provided no further verbal or written statements." The court noted that neither a defendant's pre-arrest silence nor post-arrest, pre–*Miranda* warnings silence may be used as substantive evidence of guilt, though either or both may be used to impeach the defendant by suggesting that his or her prior silence is inconsistent with statements made at trial. A defendant's post-arrest, post–*Miranda* warnings silence, however, may not be used for any purpose. Here, the defendant testified after the officer, so the State could not use the officer's statement for impeachment. Also, the officer's testimony was admitted as substantive evidence during the State's case in chief.

Use of Evidence Obtained as the Result of a *Miranda* Violation (page 637)

UNITED STATES SUPREME COURT (page 637)

Bobby v. Dixon, 132 S. Ct. 26, 28 (2011). The Court ruled that a federal appellate court erroneously concluded that a state supreme court ruling affirming the defendant's murder conviction was contrary to or involved an unreasonable application of clearly established federal law. The defendant and an accomplice murdered the victim, obtained an identification card in the victim's name, and sold the victim's car. An officer first spoke with the defendant during a chance encounter when the defendant was voluntarily at the police station for completely unrelated reasons. The officer gave the defendant *Miranda* warnings and asked to talk to him about the victim's disappearance. The defendant declined to answer questions without his lawyer and left. Five days later, after receiving information that the defendant had sold the victim's car and forged his name, the defendant was arrested for forgery and was interrogated. Officers decided not to give the defendant *Miranda* warnings for fear that he would again refuse to speak with them. The defendant admitted to obtaining an identification card in the victim's name but claimed ignorance about the victim's disappearance. An officer told the defendant that "now is the time to say" whether he had any involvement in the murder because "if [the accomplice] starts cutting a deal over there, this is kinda like, a bus leaving. The first one that gets on it is the only one that's gonna get on." When the defendant continued to deny knowledge of the victim's disappearance, the interrogation ended. That afternoon the accomplice led the police to the victim's body, saying that the defendant told him where it was. The defendant was brought back for questioning. Before questioning began, the defendant said that he heard they had found a body and asked whether the accomplice was in custody. When the police said that the accomplice was not in custody, the defendant replied, "I talked to my attorney, and I want to tell you what happened." Officers read him *Miranda* rights and obtained a signed waiver of those rights. At this point, the defendant admitted to murdering the victim. The defendant's confession to murder was admitted at trial, and the defendant was convicted of, among other things, murder and sentenced to death. After the state supreme court affirmed, the defendant filed for federal habeas relief. The district court denied relief, but a federal appellate court reversed.

The Supreme Court found that the federal appellate court erred in three respects. First, it erred by concluding that federal law clearly established that police could not speak to the defendant when five days earlier he had refused to speak to them without his lawyer. The defendant was not in custody during the chance encounter, and no law says that a person can invoke his or her *Miranda* rights anticipatorily, in a context other than custodial interrogation. Second, the federal appellate court erroneously ruled that police violated the Fifth Amendment by urging the defendant to "cut a deal" before his accomplice did so. No precedent holds that this common police tactic is unconstitutional. Third, the federal appellate court erroneously concluded that the state supreme court unreasonably applied *Oregon v. Elstad,* 470 U.S. 298 (1985), when it ruled that the defendant's second confession was voluntary. As the state supreme court explained, the defendant's statements were voluntary. During the first interrogation, he received several breaks, was given water and offered food, and was not abused or threatened. He freely acknowledged that he forged the victim's name and had no difficulty denying involvement with the victim's disappearance. Prior to his second interrogation, the defendant made an unsolicited declaration that he had spoken with his attorney and wanted to tell the police what happened. Then, before giving his confession, the defendant received *Miranda* warnings and signed a waiver-of-rights form. The state court recognized that the defendant's first interrogation involved an intentional *Miranda* violation but concluded that the breach of *Miranda* procedures did not involve actual compulsion, and thus there was no reason to suppress the later, warned confession. The federal appellate court erred by concluding that *Missouri v. Seibert,* 542 U.S. 600 (2004), mandated a different result. The nature of the interrogation here was different from that in *Seibert.* Here, the Court explained, the defendant denied involvement in the murder and then after *Miranda* warnings were given changed his mind and confessed (in *Seibert* the defendant confessed both times). Additionally, the Court noted, in contrast to *Seibert,* the two interrogations at issue here did not occur in one continuum.

Fifth Amendment Issues and Court-Ordered Mental Examinations (page 642)

Kansas v. Cheever, 134 S. Ct. 596, 601 (2013). The Court ruled that the Fifth Amendment does not prohibit the government from introducing evidence from a court-ordered mental evaluation of a criminal defendant to rebut that defendant's presentation of expert testimony in support of a defense of voluntary intoxication. It explained:

> [We hold] that where a defense expert who has examined the defendant testifies that the defendant lacked the requisite mental state to commit an offense, the prosecution may present psychiatric evidence in rebuttal. . . . Any other rule would undermine the adversarial process, allowing a defendant to provide the jury, through an expert operating as proxy, with a one-sided and potentially inaccurate view of his mental state at the time of the alleged crime.

The Court noted that "admission of this rebuttal testimony harmonizes with the principle that when a defendant chooses to testify in a criminal case, the Fifth Amendment does not allow him to refuse to answer related questions on cross-examination."

II. Lineups and Other Identification Procedures (page 664)

Due Process Review of Identification Procedures (page 665)

Generally (page 665)

UNITED STATES SUPREME COURT (page 665)

Perry v. New Hampshire, 132 S. Ct. 716, 721 (2012). The Court ruled that the Due Process Clause does not require a preliminary judicial inquiry into the reliability of an eyewitness identification when the identification was not procured under unnecessarily suggestive circumstances arranged by law enforcement. New Hampshire police received a call reporting that an African-American male was trying to break into cars parked in the lot of the caller's apartment building. When an officer responding to the call asked eyewitness Nubia Blandon to describe the man, Blandon, who was standing in her apartment building just outside the open door to her apartment, pointed to her kitchen window and said that the man she saw breaking into a car was standing in the parking lot, next to a police officer. The defendant Perry, who was that person, was arrested. About a month later, when the police showed Blandon a photographic array that included a picture of Perry and asked her to point out the man who had broken into the car, she was unable to identify Perry. At trial Perry unsuccessfully moved to suppress Blandon's identification on the ground that admitting it would violate due process. The Supreme Court began by noting that an identification infected by improper police influence is not automatically excluded. Instead, the Court explained, the trial judge at a pretrial proceeding must screen the evidence for reliability. If there is a very substantial likelihood of irreparable misidentification, the judge must exclude the evidence at trial. But, it continued, if the indicia of reliability are strong enough to outweigh the corrupting effect of the police-arranged suggestive circumstances, the identification evidence ordinarily will be admitted, and the jury will ultimately determine its worth. In this case, Perry asked the Court to extend pretrial screening for reliability to cases in which the suggestive circumstances were not arranged by law enforcement officers because of the grave risk that mistaken identification will yield a miscarriage of justice. The Court declined to do so, ruling: "When no improper law enforcement activity is involved . . . it suffices to test reliability through the rights and opportunities generally designed for that purpose, notably, the presence of counsel at postindictment lineups, vigorous cross-examination, protective rules of evidence, and jury instructions on both the fallibility of eyewitness identification and the requirement that guilt be proved beyond a reasonable doubt."

NORTH CAROLINA COURT OF APPEALS (page 667)

State v. Jackson, ___ N.C. App. ___, 748 S.E.2d 50, 57 (2013). The court ruled that an out-of-court show-up identification was not impermissibly suggestive. Officers told a victim that they "believed they had found the suspect." The victim was then taken to where the defendant was standing in a front yard with officers. With a light shining on the defendant while he was standing in the yard, the victim (who was in a patrol car) identified the defendant as the perpetrator. For reasons discussed in the opinion, the court concluded that the show-up possessed sufficient aspects of reliability to outweigh its suggestiveness.

State v. Stowes, ___ N.C. App. ___, 727 S.E.2d 351 (2012). In a robbery trial, the court of appeals found no plain error in the trial court's determination that a photo lineup was not impermissibly suggestive. The defendant argued that the photo lineup was impermissibly suggestive because one of the officers administering the procedure was involved in the investigation and because that officer may have made unintentional movements or displayed body language which could have influenced the eyewitness. The court noted that the eyewitness (an employee of the store that was robbed) was 75 percent certain of his identification; the investigating officer's presence was the only irregularity in the identification procedure. The eyewitness did not describe any suggestive actions on the part of the investigating officer, and there was no testimony from other officers to indicate such. Also, the lineup was conducted within days of the crime. Finally, the perpetrator was in the store for forty-five to fifty minutes and spoke with the employee several times.

State v. Watkins, ___ N.C. App. ___, 720 S.E.2d 844 (2012). The court ruled that a pretrial show-up was not impermissibly suggestive. The robbery victim had ample opportunity to view the defendant at the time of the crime, and there was no suggestion that the description of the perpetrator given by the victim to the police officer was inaccurate. During the show-up, the victim stood in close proximity to the defendant, and the defendant was illuminated by spotlights and a flashlight. The victim stated that he was "sure" that the defendant was the perpetrator, both at the scene and in court. Also, the time interval between the crime and the show-up was relatively short.

State v. Jones, 216 N.C. App. 225, 233 (2011). The court of appeals ruled that the trial court's admission of photo identification evidence did not violate the defendant's right to due process. The day after a break-in at her house, one of the victims, a high school student, became upset in school. Her mother was called to school and brought along the student's sister, who was also present when the crime occurred. After the student told the principal about the incident, the principal took the student, her sister, and her mother into his office and showed the sisters photographs from the North Carolina Sex Offender Registry website to identify the perpetrator. Both youths identified the perpetrator from one of the pictures. The mother then contacted the police, and the defendant was eventually arrested. At trial both youths identified the defendant as the perpetrator. The court rejected the defendant's argument that the principal acted as an agent of the State when he showed the youths the photos, finding that his actions "were more akin to that of a parent, friend, or other concerned citizen offering to help the victim of a crime." Because the principal was not a state actor when he presented the photographs, the defendant's due process rights were not implicated in the identification. Even if the principal was a state actor and the procedure used was unnecessarily suggestive, the procedure did not give rise to a substantial likelihood of irreparable misidentification given the circumstances of the identification, the court found. Finally, because the photo identification evidence was properly admitted, the trial court also properly admitted the in-court identifications of defendant.

Statutory Procedures Involving Lineups (page 668)

State v. Stowes, ___ N.C. App. ___, ___, 727 S.E.2d 351, 358 (2012). While the court of appeals ruled that the trial court did not commit plain error by granting the defendant relief under the Eyewitness Identification Reform Act (EIRA), it did not exclude evidence of a pretrial identification. The trial court found that an EIRA violation occurred because one of the officers administering the identification procedure was involved in the investigation. The court of appeals concluded: "We are not persuaded that the trial court committed plain error by granting Defendant all other available remedies under EIRA, rather than excluding the evidence."

Chapter 6

Rules of Evidence in Criminal Cases

Chapter 6

Rules of Evidence in Criminal Cases

Constitutional and Related Statutory Issues (page 684)

Constitutional Duty to Provide Evidence Materially Favorable to a Defendant; Related Statutory Obligations (page 684)

Footnote 106 (page 684)

In *Smith v. Cain,* 132 S. Ct. 627 (2012), the United States Supreme Court ruled that the notes of the lead police investigator concerning interviews with a State's witness were material and that the State's failure to disclose them entitled the defendant to a new trial because the witness's testimony was the only evidence linking the defendant to the murder, the notes strongly impeached the witness's identification of the defendant as a perpetrator and directly conflicted with his trial testimony, and the other State's evidence was not sufficiently strong to support the conviction.

Lost or Destroyed Evidence; Related Statutory Obligations (page 684)

For a discussion of legislative changes in S.L. 2012-7 to the duty to preserve biological evidence, see John Rubin, *2012 Legislation Affecting Criminal Law and Procedure* (UNC School of Government, Aug. 17, 2012). This paper is available at www.sog.unc.edu/node/1791 by selecting the link, "2012 Legislation Affecting Criminal Law and Procedure."

Index of the Cases in the Case Summaries

Note: United States Supreme Court cases are in **bold**.